"In a landscape littered with leadership books that tinker at the margins of what really matters, Ruth Haley Barton offers us practical guidance to the core of life-changing leadership: spiritual authenticity and health. *Strengthening the Soul of Your Leadership* lays bare the ancient truth that great leadership comes from the inside out, and provides a helpful road map for examining and seeking God's transformation of that largely unexamined inner core from which true leadership proceeds. This is a powerful resource for me and my own leadership team."

GARY HAUGEN, PRESIDENT OF INTERNATIONAL JUSTICE MISSION AND AUTHOR OF *GOOD NEWS ABOUT INJUSTICE*

"A weary, waiting world cries out for God-shaped leaders who would serve more than be served, who would find power by laying down power, who would lose their lives for others. In her reflections on the life of Moses, God's radically human and holy friend, Ruth Haley Barton has given us not only a portrait of what sacrificial and redemptive leadership looks like, but has provided practice for getting there. This is a book to read alone and together. It will encourage and empower us to seek God more deeply, to listen for and embody our innate callings, to stay faithful to our solitary and even lonely journeys in community, and to love God for the long haul."

N. GORDON COSBY, COFOUNDER OF THE CHURCH OF THE SAVIOUR, WASHINGTON, D.C.

"In the same spirit in which Henri Nouwen wrote *The Return of the Prodigal Son*, Ruth Haley Barton has captured the soul of Moses and has revealed him to us as a seeker of truth, wisdom and vulnerability."

GLANDION W. CARNEY, AUTHOR OF *THE WAY OF GRACE*

"For those of us who lead, there are many fine books to hone our skills. But too few excavate our souls. Too few tell us stark truths, and serve up strong tonic, and give us hope and courage in the face of our calling's hardships and loneliness and moments of sheer tedium. Too few teach us to how to seek and find God in the maze of committee work and the darkness of criticism and the heartbreak of betrayal. This book does all that, and well. Ruth Haley Barton has kept company with Moses, a 'pragmatic' and 'visionary' leader who found that, unless God went with him, there was no place worth going. Ruth's insights will at the very least strengthen the soul of your leadership. For some, it may make the difference in whether you finish the race at all."

MARK BUCHANAN, AUTHOR OF *THE REST OF GOD* AND PASTOR OF NEW LIFE COMMUNITY CHURCH

"Ruth Haley Barton has had a huge influence on the way I walk with God and walk with others. Her books and Transforming Community have helped me begin to hold the inward life and outward life together in meaningful and sustainable ways. We don't have to choose to be either exhausted activists or isolated contemplatives, and *Strengthening the Soul of Your Leadership* offers both biblical vision and time-tested rhythms to help us become contemplatives in action. Leadership does not require losing our souls. Thank God! This book will help you live into this good news."

AARON NIEQUIST, AUTHOR OF *THE ETERNAL CURRENT*

"There are many valuable books that teach leadership as a skill or even as an art. But leadership, both in civic and in church circles, is best understood when set within a spirituality. Competence is only truly effective when it issues forth from a mature soul. What ultimately grounds sound leadership? This is what Ruth Haley Barton articulates in *Strengthening the Soul of Your Leadership*. This book does for leadership what Parker Palmer's book *To Know as We Are Known* does for education. It sets skill, competence and dedication into their proper horizon—spirituality. It is a wonderful balance of insight, faith and maturity. Ruth Haley Barton is a trustworthy mentor."

RONALD ROLHEISER, PRESIDENT OF OBLATE SCHOOL OF THEOLOGY, SAN ANTONIO, AUTHOR OF *THE HOLY LONGING*

EXPANDED EDITION

STRENGTHENING THE SOUL OF YOUR LEADERSHIP

—

Seeking God in the Crucible of Ministry

—

Foreword by GARY A. HAUGEN

RUTH HALEY BARTON

IVP Books

An imprint of InterVarsity Press
Downers Grove, Illinois

InterVarsity Press
P.O. Box 1400, Downers Grove, IL 60515-1426
ivpress.com
email@ivpress.com

Second edition ©2018 by Ruth Haley Barton
First edition ©2008 by Ruth Haley Barton

InterVarsity Press® is the book-publishing division of InterVarsity Christian Fellowship/USA®, a movement of students and faculty active on campus at hundreds of universities, colleges, and schools of nursing in the United States of America, and a member movement of the International Fellowship of Evangelical Students. For information about local and regional activities, visit intervarsity.org.

Scripture quotations, unless otherwise noted, are from the New Revised Standard Version of the Bible, copyright 1989 by the Division of Christian Education of the National Council of the Churches of Christ in the USA. Used by permission. All rights reserved.

Excerpts from Guerrillas of Grace *copyright ©1981 Ted Loder admin. Augsburg Fortress. Used by permission.*

Excerpts from My Heart in My Mouth *copyright ©2004 Ted Loder admin. Augsburg Fortress. Used by permission.*

The prayer on pp. 99-100 is from Bread of Tomorrow, *ed. Janet Morley (London: SPCK, 1992). Used by permission of the Society for Promoting Christian Knowledge.*

The prayers on pages 152-53 are 2001© The Iona Community from The Iona Abbey Worship Book, Wild Goose Publications, Glasgow.

Every effort has been made to trace and contact copyright holders for additional materials quoted in this book. The authors will be pleased to rectify any omissions in future editions if notified by copyright holders.

Cover design: David Fassett
Interior design: Cindy Kiple and Jeanna Wiggins
Cover images: gray background: © GOLDsquirrel / iStock / Getty Images Plus
        graphic tree: © CSA-Archive / Digital Vision Vectors / Getty Images
        graphic flame: © CSA-Archive / Digital Vision Vectors / Getty Images

ISBN 978-0-8308-4645-0 (print)
ISBN 978-0-8308-7417-0 (digital)

Printed in the United States of America ♾

Library of Congress Cataloging-in-Publication Data
Names: Barton, R. Ruth, 1960- author.
Title: Strengthening the soul of your leadership : seeking God in the crucible of ministry / Ruth Haley Barton ; foreword by Gary A. Haugen.
Description: Expanded Edition [edition]. | Downers Grove : InterVarsity Press, 2018. | Originally published: c2008. | Includes bibliographical references.
Identifiers: LCCN 2018012222 (print) | LCCN 2018015688 (ebook) | ISBN 9780830874170 (eBook) | ISBN 9780830846450 (hardcover : alk. paper)
Subjects: LCSH: Moses (Biblical leader) | Christian leadership—Biblical teaching. | Spiritual life—Biblical teaching.
Classification: LCC BS580.M6 (ebook) | LCC BS580.M6 B37 2018 (print) | DDC 248.8/92—dc23
LC record available at https://lccn.loc.gov/2018012222

P	23	22	21	20	19	18	17	16	15	14	13	12	11	10
Y	36	35	34	33	32	31	30	29	28	27	26	25	24	23	22

FOR MY PARENTS

Rev. Dr. Charles William Haley

and

JoAnn Neburka Haley

on their

FIFTIETH WEDDING ANNIVERSARY

JUNE 7, 2008

By your words and your example
you taught me never to stop seeking God
in the crucible of ministry

CONTENTS

On the day I called, you answered me,
you increased my strength of soul.

PSALM 138:3

Foreword

Gary A. Haugen

In October of 2004, I gave each of my colleagues at International Justice Mission two gifts: a blank leather journal with the words "8:30 Stillness" embossed on the cover and a book by Ruth Haley Barton.

As an organization, we were experiencing incredible growth on a global scale. We were bringing rescue to victims of violent injustice in the most desperate places of suffering in our world, and we did so by working directly with local law enforcement and government officials to prove that justice for the poor is possible. We were witnessing miracles from the hand of God, and it was clear that the adventure had only just begun.

In the midst of this season of tremendous growth and change, I took a sabbatical with the intention of setting apart time to talk with God about what he was doing in our midst and where we were headed as we pursued his work of justice. As I emerged from my sabbatical, I shared with our team the conviction that had grown within me and presented my colleagues with the mysteriously named "8:30 Stillness" journal and Ruth's book.

I sensed that God desired for IJM to experience more of his *presence* and his *power*. But we were not yet ready to receive it.

As an organization, we had a regular rhythm of praying together every day at 11 a.m. And yet, all too often our work would veer into prayerless striving rather than expectant abiding. We longed for transformation—in ourselves and in the lives of those we sought to serve. We longed to know more deeply the love of our good Father who leads us in transformation. And yet, we needed a more disciplined attentiveness that would ready us to receive more of God's presence and power. We needed to learn to be still, to wait on the Lord, to simply *be* with him.

The gift of the journal and Ruth's book *Invitation to Solitude and Silence* was a signpost of sorts, pointing us toward a new season. Perhaps more aptly it was a toolbox, equipping us for the journey into deeper readiness to experience God's miracles of transformation—both in the world and our souls. With the blessing of our board of directors, beginning on that day when staff received their gift of the journal and book, 8:30 a.m. was declared to be the formal beginning of every IJM workday and also a time of complete stillness for all—a time we simply call "8:30 Stillness."

Now imagine with me for a moment, a staff of high-performing lawyers, criminal investigators, social workers and professionals in Washington, DC, and offices across the developing world, rushing into the office to begin their day, faced with the task of fighting slavery, human trafficking, police abuse, and other forms of violent oppression. As these staff arrive at their desks, their first order of business is to *stop*. All phones are off. Laptops closed. No email. No meetings.

Just silence. Solitude. Stillness. For thirty minutes.

On any given day, stillness can be *hard*. Even awkward, frustrating. We come to each day like a jar of river water that has been shaken. The water is murky, impossible to see through. But as the jar sits still—unmoved— the silt and sediment begin to settle. Clearer waters emerge. So too, in the stillness that enables solitude and silence, the mud and mire of our souls begin to settle and clarity emerges. In solitude and silence, we become aware of the inner needs and desires that we bring to the day. Then we can talk to God, our good and loving Father, about what it is we actually need for that day, asking for his wisdom, his guidance, his grace to prevail.

I am utterly convinced that God works miracles of transformation in the world through miraculously transformed people. God is eager for us to be *with* him, to know his love and his goodness, even as he calls us to lead with great courage in the world around us. What we have learned is that the transformation we so long for comes when, whether we feel like it or not, we actually *show up* and choose to be still in the presence of our good God.

It doesn't matter who you are or what kind of work faces you on any given day; facing the demands that confront you and choosing to be still and wait on the Lord before rushing into action is a feat that only the Spirit of God can make possible. And yet the choice to pursue daily stillness has the potential to be, perhaps more than anything else, the very crucible for the world-altering transformation every Christ-following leader is longing for.

Ruth Haley Barton has dedicated her life to distilling the wisdom to be found within these spiritual disciplines that position us to be strengthened and renewed at the level of our souls. Her guidance has been indispensable in the body of Christ at large, but also in particular to my colleagues and me at IJM. Leaders at IJM have been well guided throughout many seasons by the companionship of this very book in your hands, *Strengthening the Soul of Your Leadership*, the assessment tool this new edition now offers (see the appendix "How Is It with Your Soul?"), and the quarterly retreat experiences Ruth leads through the Transforming Center.

Strengthening the Soul of Your Leadership, alongside Ruth's wise counsel and friendship, has ministered to the entire IJM family and to me in extraordinary ways. It is a great honor to commend this book on the occasion of its tenth anniversary. Indeed, like Ruth's leadership, the wisdom in this book will guide us into the decade ahead knowing better how to seek the restoration of our souls that can lead to the transformation of the world.

How deeply we need this restoration and transformation, and all the more as we move further into the work of the kingdom and the promise of Jesus that he is, with us, making all things new.

Introduction

And what do you benefit if you

gain the whole world but lose your own soul?

Is anything worth more than your soul?

MATTHEW 16:26 NLT

This is a book about the soul—your soul, my soul and the soul of our leadership.

When I refer to the soul, I am not talking about some ill-defined, amorphous, soft-around-the-edges sort of thing. I am talking about the part of you that is most real—the very essence of you that God knew before he brought you forth in physical form, the part that will exist after your body goes into the ground. This is the "you" that exists beyond any role you play, any job you perform, any relationship that seems to define you, or any notoriety or success you may have achieved. It is the part of you that longs for more of God than you have right now, the part that may, even now, be aware of "missing" God amid the challenges of life in ministry.

Jesus indicates that it is possible to gain the whole world but lose your own soul. If he were talking to us as Christian leaders today, he might point out that it is possible to gain the world of ministry success and lose your own soul in the midst of it all. He might remind us that it is possible to find your soul, after so much seeking, only to lose it again.

If Jesus were speaking to us today, he might also point out that when leaders lose their souls, so do the churches and organizations they lead. "Soul slips away easily from a church or an institution," Gordon Cosby, founding pastor of Church of the Saviour in Washington, D.C., points out. "You may go to any of these places and find that the Spirit has departed and the Shekinah is gone. . . . When a local church loses its soul it begins to slip into mediocrity and is unable to give life. The average person doesn't even know when a church begins to lose its soul. It takes unusual deeper wisdom to see it, and then when we see it, it is costly beyond words to retrieve it."

Losing your soul is sort of like losing a credit card. You think it's in your wallet so you don't give it much thought until one day you reach for it and can't find it. The minute you realize it's gone, you start scrambling to find it, trying to remember when you last used it or at least had it in your possession. No matter what is going on in your life, you stop and look for it, because otherwise major damage could be done. Oh, that we would feel the same sense of urgency when we become aware that we have lost our souls!

THE BEST THING WE BRING TO LEADERSHIP

I have been in leadership roles all of my life—everything from serving in lay leadership positions in small churches to being on the pastoral staff of larger churches to my current responsibilities as cofounder and president of a not-for-profit ministry organization. I know what it is to serve under someone else's leadership and I know what it is to be the-buck-stops-here person and bear the weight of responsibility for carrying out a vision that has been given by God. Beyond my own experiences, I have spent years providing spiritual direction to individuals and groups of leaders on retreat and in their own settings, listening to their soul cries which are so similar to my own. These cries are gut-wrenching and consistent: *there has to be more to life in leadership than many of us are experiencing.*

In all this listening to my own life and to the lives of others, I have become convinced that the More that we are looking for is the transformation of our souls in the presence of God. It is what we want for ourselves and it is what we want for those we are leading. And that is exactly what this book is about. It is about the presence of God in the middle of a person's leadership. It is an exploration of the relationship between a person's private encounters with God in solitude and the call to leadership in the public arena. What difference does solitude and spiritual seeking make in the life of a leader—really? Is it a self-indulgent luxury that only those who are not very busy or not very much in demand can afford? Is the practice of solitude only relevant to a mystical few? Or is it more fundamental to spiritual leadership than that, type-A personalities and all?

That being said, this is not an answer book about leadership, because, quite frankly, I have more questions than answers these days. It's like the man who said, "I used to have no children and six theories [about parenting]. Now I have six children and no theories!" Somehow, when I was working in someone else's field (so to speak), I had lots of theories and, to be completely honest, lots of critiques. Now that I have borne the full weight of responsibility for an organization for a number of years, I have fewer theories, more questions and greater respect for others who have set out to lead toward a vision. I have discovered that it is so much harder than you think to create something out of nothing. Things happen that you never imagined would happen to you. The lines are much finer, the issues a lot grayer, the people so much harder to figure out, your own foibles so much more real, more deeply ingrained and more obvious to others than you ever knew.

However, I do know what some of the most fruitful questions are for leaders who want to continue to stay on the spiritual path amid the challenges of leadership. I know what it is like to walk into God's presence with those questions day after day, waiting on God to move or to shift something inside me while *at the same time* still needing to lead in the public arena. I know how important it is to have a spiritual guide or companion during those times when everything in us wants to get up and *do* something—anything!—rather than stay in that Presence. And I have walked the path of taking that tender, transforming soul back into the leadership arena and seeking to lead from that place, with all the risk that that involves.

A LEADER'S INVITATION TO SPIRITUAL TRANSFORMATION

Strengthening the soul of your leadership is an invitation to enter more deeply into the process of spiritual transformation and to choose to lead from that place. It is an opportunity to forge a connection between our souls and our leadership rather than experiencing them as separate arenas of our lives.

Spiritual transformation is the process by which Christ is formed in us for the glory of God, for the abundance of our own lives and for the sake of others. The biblical metaphors that are used in reference to the transformation process (the formation of the embryo in its mother's womb referred to in Galatians 4:19 and the metamorphosis [transformation] of the caterpillar into a butterfly alluded to in Romans 12:2) indicate that it is an organic process that goes far beyond mere behavioral tweaks to work deep, fundamental changes at the very core of our being. In the process of transformation the Spirit of God moves us from behaviors motivated by fear and self-protection to trust and abandonment to God; from selfishness and self-absorption to freely offering the gifts of the authentic self; from the ego's desperate attempts to control the outcomes of our lives to an ability to give ourselves over to the will of God which is often the foolishness of this world. This kind of change

> *Crucible: A place or set of circumstances*
> *where people or things are subjected to forces*
> *that test them and often make them change.*

is not something we can produce or manufacture for ourselves but it is what we most need. It is what those around us most need.

Lest we are tempted to view this as a glorified self-help project or an occasion for more activism, it is important for us to embrace spiritual transformation as a process that is full of mystery. It is a phenomenon that is outside the range of what human beings can accomplish on their own. It can only be grasped and experienced through divine intervention. God is the one who initiates and guides the process and brings it to fruition. The soul-full leader is appropriately humbled by this realization and also relieved to not have to bear the heavy weight of responsibility for changing herself or others. The soul-full leader is faithful to the one thing he can do—create the conditions that set us up for an encounter with God in the places where we need it most. To continually seek God in the crucible of ministry no matter how hard it gets.

THE LANGUAGE OF THE SOUL

As a spiritual director, my primary intent in this book is to guide you into encounters with God in the places where you need it most in the context of your leadership. Thus, you will find practice sections at the end of each chapter that are intended to guide you into an experience with God in much the same way I would guide you if we were together in spiritual direction or on retreat.

These practices will help you move into solitude and communion with God by encouraging you first of all to become quiet—which is no small thing!—and to pay attention to your breathing. This is a very simple way of calming the chaos in our souls and listening to the Spirit of God whom the Scriptures describe as the wind, the *pneuma,* the very breath of God. This Spirit is closer to us than our own breath.

As you become quieter in God's presence, the opportunity for prayer and honest communication with God opens up through the use of guided meditations and prayers that are written in poetic form. This is the language of the soul meant to draw out your soul and help you say what you need to say to God and hold you in a place of listening to what God wants to say to your soul.

Many of us leader-types are unaccustomed to the language of the soul and its quieter ways. Some reject it outright as being too "soft" or somehow fundamentally opposed to the life of an activistic leader. But the truth is that many of us have reached a place where we have acquired a lot of knowledge and know-how and we have accomplished much, but we know that something is missing. We are desperate to find our way back to some sort of intimacy with God that feeds our own souls. We long to receive a word from God that is spoken to our own hearts alone rather than being meant for public consumption. It takes practice to become conversant in the language of the soul; the practice sections are designed to help you do just that—to help you enter into the communion your soul seeks.

When you come to the practice section at the end of the chapter, think of it as being like that moment on retreat when you have received teaching and are now ready to spend time alone with God and try some things for yourself. It is the time when we say, "It is not good enough to just talk about these things. We need to practice, we need to find ways of entering in."

FINDING OURSELVES IN THE STORY

I have relied heavily on the life of Moses as a window into the different aspects of leadership in which we might learn to seek God and allow God to strengthen us to provide spiritual leadership to others. I have been drawn to the story of Moses because I have found it to be so complete in illustrating the different aspects of leadership and so unflinchingly honest about the challenges leaders experience. The story of Moses demonstrates that this journey of strengthening the soul of your leadership is not just for "contemplative pastors" or mystical writers. This journey is for leaders who have a job to do, who have places to go and people to lead. It is for all of us.

Even more importantly, I have interacted with the story of Moses because this is where I was able to find myself in the biblical story when I came closest to giving up on ministry and leadership. During that dark time, Moses taught me how to pray, how to stay faithful, how to wait, how to lead and how to let go when it was time. I don't think I would still be here doing what I'm doing if it were not for his story.

Having said that, there are also places where a New Testament perspective and the life of Christ are needed to give a fuller picture, since following Christ to the best of our understanding and ability is essential to our lives as people and as leaders. And so at times when referencing New Testament teachings and examples seemed necessary, I tried to incorporate them without being too disruptive to the flow of our interactions with Moses.

■   ■   ■

I have only one desire for this book, really, and that is that it will lead you into encounters with God that will strengthen the soul of your leadership in the places where you need it most. Truly, the best thing any of us have to bring to leadership is our own transforming selves. That is the journey I am committed to, however feebly at times, and it is the journey to which you are also being invited. So if seeking God with all of your heart, soul, mind and strength is the journey you are longing for . . . if you are willing to allow yourself to be transformed by what takes place there . . . if you are interested in forging a connection between your own journey of transformation and your leadership . . . then let us get on the path together and see where God leads.

O God of such truth as sweeps away all lies,
　　of such grace as shrivels all excuses,
　come now to find us
　　for we have lost our selves
　　　in a shuffle of disguises
　　　　and the rattle of empty words.

Let your Spirit move mercifully
　to recreate us from
　　the chaos of our lives.

We have been careless
　of our days,
　　our loves,
　　　our gifts,
　　　　our chances. . . .

Our prayer is to change, O God,
*   not out of despair of self*
*   but for love of you,*
*   and for the selves we long to become*
*   before we simply waste away.*

Let your mercy move in and through us now. . . .

Amen.

TED LODER, *MY HEART IN MY MOUTH*

1

WHEN LEADERS
LOSE THEIR SOULS

[Moses] is entrusted with all my house.

With him I speak face to face—

clearly, not in riddles;

and he beholds the form of the LORD.

NUMBERS 12:7-8

Several years ago, during an unusually intense season of ministry, I made a comment to a friend that surprised us both. Before I could censor my thoughts, I heard myself saying, "I'm tired of helping other people enjoy God; I just want to enjoy God for myself." This was both surprising and alarming, because what I was really saying was that my leadership, which usually flows from what is going on in my own soul, was at that moment disconnected from the reality of God in my own life.

It was not the first time I had noticed such slippage, nor would it be the last, but it was certainly one of the most clearly articulated! As my friend and I sat quietly together, the words of a poem written by Ted Loder came to me—a poem we had used many times in the Transforming Center to guide people into an honest moment with God. It sounded something like this: *"Holy One, there is something I wanted to tell you, but there have been errands to run, bills to pay, meetings to attend, washing to do . . . and I forget what it is I wanted to say to you, and forget what I am about or why. Oh God, don't forget me please, for the sake of Jesus Christ."*

As those words recited themselves in my mind, I realized that there was something *I* wanted to say to God but had been too busy and too out of touch with my own soul to say. What I wanted to say to God was "I miss you." This awareness came with such force that it felt like being knocked over by a wave that had been gathering strength while my back was turned.

SOMETHING'S NOT QUITE RIGHT

Such moments come to all of us—moments when our leadership feels like something we "put on" like a piece of clothing pulled out of the closet for a particular occasion rather than something that flows from a deep inner well fed by a pure source. Perhaps you have experienced this dynamic in your own way. Perhaps you are preparing to preach or lead a Bible study and you have the sinking realization that you are getting ready to exhort others in values and behaviors you are not living yourself. Maybe you are a worship leader and notice that more and more frequently you are manufacturing a display of emotion because it has been too long since you experienced any real intimacy with God. Or perhaps someone needs pastoral care and you realize that you just *don't care.* You rally your energy to go through the motions, but you know that your heart is devoid of real compassion.

In her book *Leaving Church,* former parish priest and award-winning preacher Barbara Brown Taylor describes what it was like to feel her soul slipping away. She says:

> Many of the things that were happening inside of me seemed too shameful to talk about out loud. Laid low by what was happening at Grace-Calvary, I did not have the energy to put a positive spin on anything. . . . Beyond my luminous images of Sunday mornings I saw the committee meetings, the numbing routines, and the chronically difficult people who took up a large part of my time. Behind my heroic image of myself I saw my tiresome perfectionism, my resentment of those who did not try as hard as I did, and my huge appetite for approval. I saw the forgiving faces of my family, left behind every holiday for the last fifteen years, while I went to conduct services for other people and their families.
>
> Above all, I saw that my desire to draw as near to God as I could had backfired on me somehow. Drawn to care for hurt things, I had ended up with compassion fatigue. Drawn to a life of servanthood, I had ended up a service provider. Drawn to marry the Divine Presence, I had ended up estranged. . . . Like the bluebirds that sat on my windowsills, pecking at the reflections they saw in the glass, I could not reach the greenness for which my soul longed. For years I had believed that if I just kept at it, the glass would finally disappear. Now for the first time, I wondered if I had devoted myself to an illusion.

Sometimes our sense that something is not quite right is more subtle, as it was for one young pastor who had come for spiritual direction. With keen self-awareness he observed, "I find [leadership] conferences to be very exciting on one level, but there is something darker that happens as well. Sometimes they leave me feeling competitive toward other churches and what they are accomplishing. I leave the conference feeling dissatisfied with my own situation—my own staff, my own resources, my own gifts and abilities. My ego gets ramped up to do bigger and better things, and then I go home and drive everyone crazy. Three months later, the conference notebook is on a bookshelf somewhere, and I have returned to life as usual with a vague feeling of uneasiness about my effectiveness as leader, never quite sure if I am measuring up."

This was not meant to be a critique of any particular conference; rather, he was courageously naming in God's presence and in the presence of another person what was taking place inside his soul in the context of his leadership. His desire was to hear from God in that place. He knew that if his soul was to be well, he could not afford to live his life driven blindly by unexamined inner dynamics.

HOW IS IT WITH YOUR SOUL?

When the early Wesleyan bands of Christ-followers got together in small group meetings, their first question to each other was "How is it with your soul?" This is the best possible question for us as Christian leaders in light of Jesus' warning and in light of what we witness in and around us. So how is it with your soul?

Some of us know that we are losing bits and pieces of our soul every day, and we are scared to death that we might go over the edge. Others of us are still hanging in there fairly well, but we are not sure how long we will last. All of us have watched ministry friends and colleagues endure heartbreak, failure or betrayal so profound that they left ministry and are now selling real estate.

Those of us who have been in ministry for any length of time at all are under no illusion that we are exempt from such outcomes. Even the young ones know better these days. One emerging leader wrote, "I feel the call of God to move deeper and deeper into service through preaching and leadership. At the same time I am keenly aware of what ministry is doing to the personal spiritual lives of almost everyone I know on staff or in key volunteer positions in the church. I am increasingly unsure about how one is supposed to navigate the time commitments of ministry and one's personal journey toward growth and wholeness. I find myself wondering if the two aren't mutually exclusive."

These are uncomfortable admissions, and paying attention to them requires a certain kind of courage because we don't know where such honest reflections will take us. However, if we are willing to listen to our uneasiness, it might lead us to important questions that are lurking under the surface of our Christian busyness. "How does spiritual leadership differ from other models for leadership?" we might find ourselves wondering. "And how can I be strengthened at the soul level to provide such leadership? What would it look like for me to lead more consistently from my soul—the place of my own encounter with God— rather than leading primarily from my head, my unbridled activism, or my performance-oriented drivenness? What would it be like to *find* God in the context of my leadership rather than miss God in the context of my leadership?"

THE CHALLENGE OF SPIRITUAL LEADERSHIP

The soulful leader pays attention to such inner realities and the questions that they raise rather than ignoring them and continuing the charade *or* judging himself or herself harshly and thus cutting off the possibility of deeper awareness. Spiritual leadership emerges from our willingness to stay involved with our own soul—that place where God's Spirit is at work stirring up our deepest questions and longings to draw us deeper into relationship with him. Staying involved with our soul is not narcissistic navel gazing; rather, this kind of attentiveness helps us stay on the path of becoming our true self in God—a self that is capable of an ever-deepening yes to God's call on our life.

But right away this presents us with a challenge. For one thing, the soul is a tender thing, and leadership can be very dangerous. As Parker Palmer says, "The soul is like a wild animal—tough, resilient, resourceful, savvy. It knows how to survive in hard places. But it is also shy. Just like a wild animal, it seeks safety in the dense underbrush. If we want to see a wild animal, we know that the last thing we should do is go crashing through the woods yelling for it to come out."

The settings in which many of us are trying to provide leadership are places where everyone is crashing through the woods together, harried and breathless, staying on the surface of the intellect and the ego while all things soulful flee deeper into the woods. Besides that, we know that the leader is often the one who gets shot at or voted off the island. The savvy soul knows better than to run out into a clearing, thereby giving everyone a better shot!

Beyond the challenge of coaxing the soul to show up in such a dangerous environment, there are the many challenges that present themselves once the soul does make an appearance and starts sniffing around. As we become more attentive to our environments through the eyes of the soul, we might notice tension between what the spiritual life requires and what it takes to be (or at least appear!) successful in the current cultural milieu. On our good days, we might experience these tensions as a place of paradox where creative solutions might be found, but on other days they feel like polarities that are impossible to manage.

These days (and maybe every day) there is real tension between what the human soul needs in order to be truly well and what life in leadership encourages and even requires. There is the tension between being and doing, community and cause, truth-telling and putting the right spin on things. There is the tension between the time it takes to love people and the need for expediency. There is the tension between the need for measurable goals and the difficulty of measuring that which is ultimately immeasurable by anyone but God himself.

There is the tension between the need for organizational hierarchy with all the power dynamics this creates and the mutuality and interdependence of life in community to which we as Christians are called. There is the tension between knowing how to "work the system" and entering into trustworthy relationships characterized by trust and a commitment to one another's well-being. There is the tension between the need for an easy discipleship process through which we can efficiently herd lots of people and the patient, plodding and ultimately mysterious nature of the spiritual transformation process. And then there is the challenge of knowing how to speak of these things in fruitful ways in the very inside places of power without becoming polarized in our relationships with one another.

NOT FOR THE FAINT OF HEART

Leadership that functions creatively and spiritually in the midst of paradox is not for the faint of heart. It is much easier to give in to one polarity or the other. Peter Senge notes in *The Fifth Discipline,* "Emotional tension can always be relieved by adjusting the one pole of the creative tension that is completely under our control at all times—the vision. The feelings that we dislike go away because the creative tension that was their source is reduced. Our goals are now much closer to our current reality. Escaping emotional tension is easy—the only price we pay is abandoning what we truly want, our vision." A spiritual leader is not willing to merely escape emotional tension; rather, he or she has the stamina and staying power to remain in that place of creative tension until a third way opens up that somehow honors both realities.

The temptation to compromise basic Christian values—love, community, truth-telling, confession and reconciliation, silent listening and waiting on God for discernment—for the sake of expedience is very great. In a high performance culture (both secular culture and religious), holding to deep spiritual values in the face of the pressure to perform—whether performance is measured by numbers, new buildings or the latest innovation—is one of the greatest challenges of spiritual leadership.

When I was growing up as a pastor's kid, my dad's responsibilities as a pastor were in some ways very simple. He preached on Sundays and sometimes Wednesday evenings. He visited the sick and counseled those in need of pastoral care. He sat with the elders, and they made decisions together regarding the ministries and business aspects of the church. That was about it and that was enough!

These days, the pastoral/ministry role is much more complicated. Now, in addition to those basic responsibilities, many pastors are expected to function like CEOs of large corporations. They are expected to be strategic thinkers and planners. They are expected to be good managers. They are expected to preach sermons that are culturally relevant *and* contribute expertise and innovative ideas regarding production and programming. They are expected to lead fundraisers and capital campaigns. They are expected to be skilled at interpersonal relating but also to command the attention of large crowds. Such expectations generate many places of paradox that will respond to nothing less than the tough, resourceful, savvy, resilient soul that was so hard to coax out in the first place!

The only way to begin facing these challenges is to keep seeking tenaciously after God through spiritual disciplines that keep us grounded in the presence of God at the center of our being. Solitude and silence in particular enable us to experience a place of authenticity within and to invite God to meet us there. In solitude we are rescued from relentless human striving to solve the challenges of ministry through intellectual achievements and hard work, so that we can experience the life of the Spirit guiding toward that true way that lies between one polarity and another. In silence we give up control and allow God to be God in our life rather than being a thought in our head or an illustration in a sermon. In that place of our seeking we listen for the still, small voice of God telling us who we really are and what is real from a spiritual point of view. Then we are not quite so enslaved by the demands and expectations of life in leadership.

> *The central question is, Are the leaders of the future*
>
> *truly men and women of God,*
>
> *people with an ardent desire to dwell in God's presence,*
>
> *to listen to God's voice, to look at God's beauty,*
>
> *to touch God's incarnate Word*
>
> *and to taste fully God's infinite goodness?*
>
> HENRI NOUWEN, *IN THE NAME OF JESUS*

WHAT I KNOW FOR SURE

The market is glutted with books on leadership, and many contain contradictory messages. I'm not sure anyone has the full perspective—really. But one of the things I know for sure is that those who are looking to us for spiritual sustenance need us first and foremost to be spiritual seekers ourselves. They need us to keep searching for the bread of life that feeds our own souls so that we can guide them to places of sustenance for *their* own souls. Then, rather than offering the cold stone of past devotionals, regurgitated apologetics or someone else's musings about the spiritual life, we will have bread to offer that is warm from the oven of our intimacy with God.

I often receive e-mails and questions about the "training" I received to prepare me for offering spiritual leadership through writing, teaching, retreat leadership and the work of the Transforming Center. What follows their initial question is usually an inquiry about what training I would recommend for them as they pursue a similar path. This question always gives me pause, because it was not so much the training I have received that has prepared me for what I am doing now—although I have been privileged to receive some excellent training. It is the *path* I have been on that has prepared me for the leadership I bring now. And it was my desperate seeking after God that began when I was a young leader in my early thirties that put me on this path. Each and every risky step I took with God, along with willingness to move far outside of my comfort zone, prepared me for what I do today.

As I searched I had no idea or intention that I would lead anyone else in such endeavors. In fact, my spiritual search led me to drop out of ministry at one point, and I thought my life in leadership was over. But I was so desperate for God that nothing else mattered. God eventually called me back into ministry, but it was that time of intense spiritual seeking that set everything in motion, and it is all by God's grace. Reflecting back on those early experiences reminds me every day that the most important thing I can do as a leader today is to keep seeking God in depths of my own soul—no matter what it costs.

A LEADER WITH STRENGTH OF SOUL

As my calling into leadership has deepened and the terrain has become more rugged, I have been drawn to the story of Moses, because his hard-won strength of soul forged in his private encounters with God gave him the staying power he needed for the long haul of leadership. He made it all the way to the finish line of his life in leadership not because he knew how to *think about* leadership and conceptualize it in clever ways. He lasted because he allowed his leadership challenges to *catalyze* and *draw him into* a level of reliance on God that he might not have pursued had it not been for his great need for God which he experienced most profoundly in the crucible of leadership. He literally had no place else to go!

Moses' whole life can be viewed through the lens of his private encounters with God and how his soul was strengthened through those encounters. He did not seem to have any great strategies for leadership except to seek God in solitude and then carry out what God revealed to him there. He routinely sought God out (or God sought him), there was an encounter, and then Moses did what God told him to do. For Moses, leadership was that simple!

Today we might say that that is too simplistic an approach to leadership given the complexities and the unique challenges of life in our culture. Perhaps. I, like you, have been around the leadership block too many times to accept simplistic answers to complex questions. However, I also believe that there is such a thing as the simplicity beyond the complexity, and perhaps this is a part of it.

A LEADER'S JOURNEY INTO SOLITUDE AND SILENCE

The discipline of solitude is a key discipline for all those who seek after God. It is the primary place where the leader's soul is strengthened. However, a leader's journey into solitude and silence has particular challenges. One of the reasons solitude is so challenging for leaders is that the activities and experiences associated with leadership can be very addicting. The idea that I can *do* something about this, that or the other thing feeds something in us that is voracious in its appetite. That something is the ego or the false self, which, over time, identifies itself and shores itself up with external accomplishments and achievements, roles and titles, power and prestige. Leadership roles, by their very nature, give a lot of fodder to the ego. To remove ourselves, even for a time, from the very arena where we are receiving so much of our identity can be difficult if not impossible for leaders, no matter how much mental assent we give to the idea.

Many leaders preach solitude better than they practice it, and I suspect that this may be the heart of the matter. Leaders are busy, yes. Solitude necessitates that we pull away from the demands of our lives in ministry, which is never easy and involves many logistical challenges. But I wonder if the real reason we resist actually moving into solitude may have more to do with the anxiety that comes as we pull away from that which we have allowed to define us externally. Usually we're not willing to let go of that unless we are desperate. As we discover in Moses' story, it almost always takes some level of desperation for a leader to move beyond mere dabbling in solitude and silence and into the kind of encounters with God that Moses experienced.

And so I have found myself wanting to learn more about what happened to Moses in those times alone with God and how his leadership emerged from them. I have been jealous to experience even a fraction of the Presence that kept Moses so clear about his calling. I have longed to be as tenacious as Moses in battling it out with God rather than giving up (or dreaming about giving up) when the going gets tough. I have asked God for the kind of courage and staying power that enabled Moses to stay faithful over the long haul of leadership. And I have cried out for the grace to live with my own limitations and imperfections, as Moses did, and not be completely derailed by them.

Moses' encounters with God in solitude were clearly his lifeline, his only means of survival. When he got to the end of his life, he was described as the greatest prophet in Israel, whom the Lord knew face to face. He did not achieve his vision the way he had envisioned it, but he knew God and God knew him—which is perhaps the greatest achievement of all. These days, that is all I want.

PRACTICE

Someone has said, "You'd be surprised at what your soul wants to say to God."

For those of us who are in leadership, it is often hard to find space that is quiet enough and safe enough for the soul to be as honest as it needs to be. We don't often take the time to sit quietly by the base of the tree of our

own lives and wait for the wild animal we seek to put in an appearance.
Here is an invitation to sit quietly for a few moments for the sole purpose
of allowing your soul to say what it needs to say to God. Don't try to force
anything or work hard to make something happen. The soul runs from
such attempts. Just sit quietly in God's presence and see what shows itself.
This may take time but when your soul has finally said that thing that it
has been waiting to say, you will know. If you sit long enough, you might
also be surprised at what God wants to say to your soul.

■　■　■

Holy One,
there is something I wanted to tell you
but there have been errands to run,
　　bills to pay,
　　　arrangements to make,
　　　　meetings to attend,
　　　　　friends to entertain,
　　　　　　washing to do . . .
and I forget what it is I wanted to say to you,
and mostly I forget what I'm about,
　　or why.
O God,
don't forget me, please,
for the sake of Jesus Christ. . . .

O Father in Heaven,
perhaps you've already heard what I wanted to tell you.
What I wanted to ask is
　　forgive me,
　　　heal me,
　　　　increase my courage, please.
Renew in me a little of love and faith,

and a sense of confidence,
and a vision of what it might mean
to live as though you were real,
and I mattered,
and everyone was sister and brother.

What I wanted to ask in my blundering way is
don't give up on me,
don't become too sad about me,
but laugh with me,
and try again with me,
and I will with you, too.

TED LODER, *GUERRILLAS OF GRACE*

2

WHAT LIES BENEATH

One day, after Moses had grown up, . . . he saw

an Egyptian beating a Hebrew, one of his kinsfolk.

He looked this way and that, and seeing no one

he killed the Egyptian and hid him in the sand. . . .

Moses fled from Pharoah. He settled in the

land of Midian, and sat down by a well.

EXODUS 2:11-12, 15

Moses was destined to be a leader. When you are raised as the son of a princess, you are groomed to lead. You are scrutinized and evaluated regarding your capacity to lead. Expectations are high.

But Moses had a problem. He was not an Egyptian by blood, nor was he related by blood to the royal princess who was raising him. He had been adopted by Pharaoh's daughter after she rescued him from a basket which she found floating among the reeds near where she was bathing. His mother had placed him there in a desperate attempt to spare him from Pharaoh's murderous instructions to kill all boy babies born to the Hebrews. With Moses' sister stationed nearby to keep watch, the princess found him and had pity on him. Moses' sister came out of her hiding place and offered to find a Hebrew woman to nurse him. The rest, as they say, is history. In a wonderful reversal, Moses ended up being nursed by his own mother, and then when he was old enough, his mother brought him back to Pharaoh's daughter, who raised him as her son. Pharaoh's daughter named him Moses, reflecting her experience of drawing him out of the water.

Even though this was a fairly happy ending and one that contains much evidence of God's grace, it still made for a convoluted childhood by today's therapeutic standards! While it is good to be careful not to go too far in imposing contemporary meanings on ancient texts, we might at least acknowledge that Moses' early childhood experiences were quite traumatic by any standard. He was born into an environment that was highly unsafe and volatile for children. He was abandoned by his mother, even though it was for the best of reasons. He was then reunited with his birth family only to be returned to his adoptive family later on. He was raised in a pagan environment that was fundamentally different from the environment in which he had spent his early years, an environment that prohibited him from living and worshiping with his family and his fellow Hebrews according to the traditions of his own heritage. He lived between two worlds and yet was not fully at home in either place.

No matter how you look at it, this was a very difficult situation for any child to be raised in and even harder to come to grips with in one's adult life. Moses probably had a bit of a chip on his shoulder, because he always had something to prove. As an outsider both among his own people and among the Egyptians who had raised him, he probably wrestled every day with issues related to his identity. Should he fit into the environment in which he had been raised and follow the path marked out for him there? Or should he identify with his own people and try to make it by those rules instead? Neither one was a very good choice. Either one would bring about emptiness and loss.

We can be fairly certain that Moses developed some pretty good coping mechanisms for dealing with the pain of his situation, as all human beings do. All of us develop ways of adjusting and staying safe in the midst of whatever danger or difficulty is present in our environment. We develop these patterns before we are conscious that we are doing so, and they become very normal for us. Because these patterns are formed unconsciously while we are still young, as adults we have little conscious awareness of these adaptations until they start to hamper our current relationships and no longer serve the journey that God is inviting us to.

It appears that one of Moses' coping mechanisms was to repress his anger since he had nowhere to go with it. But he also used that anger to "power up" in relation to others and to control situations that seemed out of control. One day his anger—anger that had probably been building for quite a long time—got the best of him and everything exploded. On this day he "went out to his people"—a poignant phrase! Because he was not free to live with his own people, the best he could do was visit from time to time. My guess is that the longing to fully fit somewhere— to stay and be at home—was deep and profound.

We don't know if this was the first time Moses had gotten a glimpse of how his people were living, but this time it certainly struck a nerve, a nerve he might not have known was so sensitive. When he saw an

Egyptian abusing a Hebrew, his anger overwhelmed him, and he killed the Egyptian. Then he tried to hide his sin by burying the body in the sand. This reactive and out-of-control response was a snapshot of Moses' leadership before solitude.

The very next day, when he visited his people again and tried to help them by refereeing a fight between two Hebrews, they would not have it. They had seen Moses' violent attempts at "helping" and were quite cynical about it. Their reaction to his unrefined and undisciplined leadership was, "Who made you a ruler and a judge over us? Do you mean to kill me as you killed the Egyptian?" (Exodus 2:14). And Moses was afraid, as well he should have been. He was afraid that he would be found out, that he would be seen for who he really was. What had been present under the surface of his life was now *on the surface,* and it could no longer be ignored.

> *A leader is a person who must take special*
>
> *responsibility for what's going on inside him- or herself,*
>
> *inside his or her consciousness,*
>
> *lest the act of leadership create more harm than good.*
>
> PARKER PALMER, "LEADING FROM WITHIN"

TAKING OURSELVES OUT OF THE ACTION

Recently I took a trip to Florida for a week by myself—to rest, walk the beach and swim in the ocean every day. I knew it was a bit risky to swim alone, and on occasion it crossed my mind that if I didn't come out of the ocean on any given day, no one would have known—at least not for a day or two. That thought didn't bother me too much until one day when the danger became more real.

On this day, I was swimming and floating in the surf when a fisherman came running down the beach yelling, "Get out of the water! Get out of the water!" I swam as hard as I could toward the shore, and when I found my footing I ran—heart pounding—the rest of the way. As soon as I was safely on shore, I turned around and saw a long, black shadow about six to eight feet long gliding under the surface of the water right where I had just emerged. Breathlessly I asked the fisherman, "Was it a shark?" He said, "No, it's a saltwater crocodile!" Then he kept running down the beach yelling at people to get out of the water.

I had never heard of saltwater crocodiles, but the people gathered on the beach seemed to know something about these underwater creatures. They said that there had never been a saltwater crocodile reported in these parts before, and they mused about how it had gotten there. Was it through the intercoastal waterway, they wondered, or one of the nearby passes? Later that day I did return to swimming—albeit a little more cautiously—and found out from those who knew about such things that saltwater crocodiles are one of the most dangerous creatures in the ocean.

The moral of the story as it relates to leadership is this: *what lies beneath the surface—of the ocean or our lives—really matters.* Whether I know something is there or not is in some ways irrelevant. My awareness of it or lack of awareness doesn't make it any less real. It doesn't much matter whether I have ever heard of what is lurking beneath the surface or whether I believe that such things exist. The point is that there *are* things lurking under the surface, and it could even be that others are seeing these things though I am not. If, by God's grace, we become aware of the dark creatures lurking below, the best thing we can do is to get out of the water—fast!

This is exactly what Moses did when he got a glimpse of the dark thing that had been lurking under the surface of his consciousness and was starting to surface so powerfully. That one glimpse of the destructive power of his raw and unrefined leadership was so frightening to Moses that he fled into solitude. He did not walk. He did not jog. He did not take time to figure out what it was or to put his affairs in order. He *fled* into solitude. He said, in effect, "This part of me, if left as it is, will be no good for anyone." Yes, he ran because he was afraid of Pharaoh, but oftentimes it is the fear of being found out or the actual experience of being found out that alerts us to what lies beneath. It actually places us on the path of self-discovery and (hopefully) forces us to do whatever work we need to do to take more responsibility for the dark forces that have propelled our bad behavior.

Often it takes something of this magnitude for a leader to move beyond mere dabbling in solitude to a more substantive experience. There is some behavioral pattern, something unresolved, something out of control enough, something destructive enough, that we say, "I must go into solitude with this." We thought we had kept it fairly well hidden. We thought we could manage it or at least keep its destructive nature fairly private, but now here it is—out there for all to see—and it is wreaking havoc on our attempts to accomplish something good.

We must not ignore this moment when it comes. It is one way that the leader's journey into solitude and silence begins. If such a moment comes early on as it did for Moses, thanks be to God. It is by God's grace that we are given the opportunity to face ourselves before the stakes are any higher. If it comes later on—as it does for most of us—then thanks be to God. It means that God is at work, leading us to greater freedom than we have yet known. In such moments, God's call to us is to find a way to do what Moses did—to leave our life in the company of others at least for a time, to let go of all of our attempts to fix whatever needs fixing "out there," to leave whatever hope we had of leading people somewhere, and to believe that what needs to be done in the deep interior places of our life is the most important work to be done right now. In fact, to try to press on without paying attention to whatever it is that is bubbling up from way down deep is the most dangerous thing we could do.

SETTLING INTO OURSELVES

The first thing solitude required of Moses was taking some time to settle down. He settled in Midian, a place that was far from public view, far from the places where the most painful parts of his life had occurred, far from the place of his greatest mistake so far. The work that was needed in his life required time, space and a great deal of privacy.

The Scriptures go into further detail by telling us that he *sat down by a well*. The well has long been a metaphor for the soul, the hidden riches and depths of the human person. In Jungian psychology, water is an image of the hidden world, a symbol of the unconscious containing life that is invisible and yet contains wrecks and treasures for the finding. In the spiritual writings of Teresa of Ávila, water represents not only the depths of the human person but also the deep interior presence of God. The metaphor of water and wells is significant in scriptural passages as well. Jesus refers to himself as the living water and the spiritual person as one from whom springs of living water flow because they are connected with the Source of that living water deep within.

Moses sits down beside a real well, yes, but the well can be seen as a metaphor for his own depths and the depths of God. In settling down by the depths of his own soul he begins to be in touch with something more honest and substantive than the patterns that produced his angry outburst. Almost immediately—and without Moses even being aware of it—solitude begins to do its good work. And that's the way it is. Solitude will do its good work whether we know what we are doing or not.

One of the primary functions of solitude is to settle into ourselves in God's presence. This is not easy and it takes time. But it is the answer to the heart cry that erupts when we have been distracted for too long by surface concerns. "I have lost myself!" we cry. Solitude is the only way to find ourselves again. And the longer we have been lost to ourselves, caught up with external stimulation, the longer it takes to find our way home again.

At this point in the solitude journey we need to be careful of ourselves and our expectations. Most of what happens in solitude is happening under the surface, and God is doing it. Just as most of what's happening in the ocean is under the surface and most of what's happening to a seed in winter is under the earth, so the most important stuff that is happening to the human soul in solitude is happening under the surface, where only God knows about it. This was certainly true for Moses. The next time we see him exercising leadership, he is starting to use it for good in more effective ways. The strong sense of justice that is essential to his nature is still there, but this time he uses it to come to the defense of some shepherd girls who are being threatened by unruly shepherds. This time Moses is truly helpful—he defends the shepherd girls and helps them water their sheep—and he exercises restraint. This time he accomplishes justice without killing anyone—a real improvement! His withdrawal from a more public existence and the settling that has taken place are already paying off.

WHEN I WANT TO DO GOOD

In Gary McIntosh and Samuel Rima's *Overcoming the Dark Side of Leadership,* they explore the phenomenon of prominent Christian leaders who have been brought down by their unattended "dark side." These writers expose the subtle dysfunctions that drive Christian leaders but often go undetected and unchallenged until it is too late. They articulate what we have already noted in the life of Moses. "The dark side is actually a natural result of human development. It is the inner urges, compulsions, and dysfunctions of our personality that often go unexamined or remain unknown to us until we experience an emotional explosion or some other significant problem that causes us to search for a reason why. At times the dark side seems to leap on us unexpectedly but in reality it has slowly crept up on us . . . it has been a lifetime in the making."

Moses' leadership, before it had been refined by his encounters with God in solitude, was raw, undisciplined, violent and destructive to those who were in its path. Like so many of us as leaders, Moses' natural gifting was at the mercy of his unresolved past and the unexamined emotional patterns that drove him. He is a flesh-and-blood example of Paul's statement in Romans 7:21: "I find it to be a law that when I want to do what is good, evil lies close at hand."

All of us have a shadow side to our leadership. Most of us start out with a desire to do good things and to make a difference; however, as McIntosh and Rima point out, "the personal insecurities, feelings of inferiority, and need for parental approval (among other dysfunctions) that compel people to become successful leaders are often the very same issues that precipitate their failure."

What Paul is saying and what Moses' life illustrates is that when we set out to do good but carry out our attempts without the discipline of attending to what lies beneath and opening it up in God's presence, evil is always close at hand. The raw gift of leadership may be there—as it certainly was for Moses—along with a strong sense of what is right and what we think needs to be done in this world. But our leadership cannot be a force for good if it is not being refined by the rigors of true solitude, that place where God is at work beyond what we are able to do for ourselves or would even know how to do for ourselves.

In one sense, Moses was fortunate that his dark side was exposed so early in his development as a leader—when the stakes were not as high as they would be later on and when fewer people were affected. Perhaps God knew that if his penchant toward murderous rages had surfaced while the Israelites were hanging on by a thread in the wilderness, the whole mission might have been lost. Facing his dark side and moving into solitude with it was one of the most important things he could have done to prepare for what was ahead. Moses did what we all must do when such awareness breaks in: we must find a way to take our whole self into God's presence— shadow side and all—and wait for solitude to do its good work.

This is a leader's invitation to freedom from the inner bondage of being subject to the deeply patterned responses that were helpful to us at one time but could cripple us now in what we are being called to do.

This is a call to liberation that we are often able to hear only when we have finally become desperate enough to consider a radical departure from life as we know it so that we can be made well. Only those whom God has freed at this level are prepared to lead others into the freedom that they seek. Only those who have been brave enough to ride their own monsters of anger and greed, jealousy and narcissism, fear and violence all the way down to the bottom will find a truer energy with which to lead. Only those who have faced their own dark side can be trusted to lead others toward the Light.

This is where true *spiritual* leadership begins. Everything that comes before is something else.

PRACTICE

Your invitation to solitude in the midst of your life in leadership need not be as dramatic or traumatic as it was for Moses. The impetus might be a longing that just won't go away—a sense of missing God—that all the accolades of ministry cannot fill. It might be a level of exhaustion that no one else knows about—yet. It might be an awareness of a sin pattern that you used to be able to control but now is pressing in on you with greater urgency. It might be feelings of hopelessness or depression that no one else sees and yet are a dark current running under the surface of your busy life, threatening to pull you under. It doesn't really matter how the invitation comes; what matters is that you say yes.

At the close of this chapter, take a few minutes to sit quietly in God's presence and notice what it is that is drawing you into solitude in the midst of your life in leadership. Why this? Why now?

Try not to fight the awareness that comes or talk yourself out of what you are experiencing. If, like Moses, what you see causes you to be afraid, let yourself experience that fear (or that sadness or whatever it is) as part of the energy that will enable you to do what you need to do. Take at least ten minutes to sit quietly in God's presence with your growing awareness of what is drawing you into solitude at this time. Allow yourself to experience the hope that comes with knowing that there is a safe place for you to acknowledge what is true about you and to wait for God's action in your life.

■   ■   ■

O God,
let something essential happen to me,
  something more than interesting
    or entertaining
      or thoughtful.
O God,
let something essential happen to me,
  something awesome,
    something real.
Speak to my condition, Lord,
and change me somewhere inside where it matters . . .
Let something happen in me
which is my real self, God.

TED LODER, *GUERRILLAS OF GRACE*

3

THE PLACE
OF OUR OWN
CONVERSION

[Moses] named [his son] Gershom; for he said,
"I have been an alien residing in a foreign land."

EXODUS 2:22

Moses remained in a solitary, nonpublic existence for a long time. It was as if—in some deep and fundamental way—he just let go. He let go of his dreams of fixing anything, helping anyone or even living among his people. Instead, he received what was given. He was offered a home in Midian, and so he settled there. He was given a wife, and so he took her as his own. He fathered a son, and it became a touchstone in his life, an opportunity to name something about himself with more courage and realism than ever before. When his son was born, he named him Gershom because "I have been an alien residing in a foreign land" (Exodus 2:22).

This was a profound admission. It had taken a very long time, but finally Moses was able to acknowledge what was underneath the behavior that had gotten him where he was. He was finally able to admit that all his life he had struggled with his identity and he was mad as hell about it. People around him were confused about who he was because *he* was confused about who he was. His relationship with Zipporah was a case in point. After Moses helped her water her sheep, she brought Moses home to meet her father and introduced him as an Egyptian. Moses didn't even bother to correct her. He was so accustomed to being unclear about his identity and adapting himself to whatever situation he found himself in that he just kept quiet and let people believe what they wanted.

But one day, after he had been in the wilderness long for enough for solitude to do its good work, he was able to claim his greatest pain and brokenness. It is doubtful that Moses knew exactly what was going on in that wilderness place. Most of us don't when we first begin entering in. But solitude does its work whether we have any cognitive understanding of it or not. Just as the physical law of gravity ensures that sediment swirling in a jar of muddy river water will eventually settle and the water will become clear, so the spiritual law of gravity ensures that the chaos of the human soul will settle if it sits still long enough. So, after weeks and months in solitude, the chaos in Moses' soul settled a bit. He began to make sense of his own history, and he was finally able to say, "This is who I am. The experience of living as an alien in a foreign land is what has shaped me."

Finally he had come home to himself.

All of us have need of this kind of homecoming in which we claim our experiences as our own and acknowledge the ways they have shaped us. Then we are in a position to take responsibility for ourselves rather than being driven by our unconscious patterns of manipulating and controlling reality. As Parker Palmer observes, "A leader is a person who must take special responsibility for what's going on inside him or her self, inside his or her consciousness, lest the act of leadership create more harm than good."

Taking responsibility for oneself may well be more demanding than taking responsibility for a congregation or an organization! Whether it happens early or late, it is crucial to our capacity to lead spiritually.

WHEN OUR PATTERNS GET THE BEST OF US

Former President Bill Clinton is a well-known present-day example of how our unwillingness to face the unresolved pains of our past can diminish our current effectiveness as leaders. It is common knowledge that Clinton's growing-up years were spent in a home with an alcoholic stepfather who was violent, abusive and unfaithful to his mother. By his own admission, Billy's job as a young boy was to take care of the rest of the family and to act like the "father" in the situation. This was a heavy and unnatural weight for a young boy to carry, but even so, when asked about his early life Clinton has insisted that he had a good life and a normal childhood.

A more accurate assessment of the situation offered by a psychologist provides what is perhaps a more realistic perspective:

The perception that he had a normal childhood indicates Clinton's deeply ingrained denial of his youthful experiences. . . . But one must grasp his deep-seated level of denial when he describes a childhood of repeated episodes of abandonment; parental alcoholism; marriage of his mother; divorce; remarriage; his stepfather's death, violence directed at his mother, brother and himself; his second stepfather's death; gunshots discharged in his home as a normal life. A true description of Clinton's childhood would be: chaotic and highly abnormal.

Apparently, Clinton's ability to deny what was real and to describe his childhood as something it was not developed at an early age, and it helped him survive psychologically. It is what he needed to believe in order to cope with his situation; however, the long-term result was that he developed unconscious patterns of denial that did not serve him well as an adult and as a leader. When Clinton, as president of the United States, responded to accusations about drug use, draft dodging and marital infidelity with this deeply patterned denial of reality, it was disastrous to his credibility and effectiveness as a leader. He was likable but he was not trustworthy.

While it is tempting to sit back and make smug judgments about a leader whose foibles have become very public, let us be quick to acknowledge that none of us are immune to the results of being born as a tender self needing to find ways to protect ourselves from the wounding elements in our environment. Some of us are just better at hiding it than others! But we are no longer children. As adults on the spiritual journey, we have a responsibility to name and claim these ineffectual and destructive patterns as our own, as one step toward the repatterning that must take place if we are to live into the love, trust, and courage that God is inviting us to. Even though our coping mechanisms and sin patterns may be more subtle than the ones described here, they are just as detrimental.

A LOOK IN THE MIRROR
Part of the reason that leadership is a crucible is that if we stick with it

past the initial euphoria, the demands of long-term leadership usually push us to a place where our patterns are clearly revealed. The demands of ministry keep our face pressed up against the mirror until we are able to acknowledge the hidden dynamics that are driving us:

- A leader whose father was stern and demanding and who never heard a full and unconditional "I love you" finds himself on a performance treadmill, always working unconsciously to gain approval and a sense of self. The drivenness that results can become a debilitating source of exhaustion.

- A leader who was raised in a punishing environment where there was an inordinate emphasis on "being good" and behaving develops perfectionist tendencies that keep feelings of shame and inadequacy at bay. The longer this perfectionism remains unacknowledged, the more likely she is to hurt herself and others with unrealistic expectations and ideals.

- A leader who experienced not being wanted at conception or birth learns to doubt his basic self-worth and develops patterns of hiding his real self from others. This type of leader remains distant and aloof because that seems easier than risking more rejection. It prevents him from entering into authentic community, which is essential to spiritual leadership.

- A leader who has experienced profound loneliness, abandonment or loss learns to keep busy as a way of avoiding the deep feelings that such experiences bring. While staying busy, she is able to maintain a superficial peace; however, over time it becomes obvious that she is unable to "stay in the room" and deal honestly and rigorously with the most challenging issues that need to be faced.

- A leader who has lived with significant emotional or physical deprivation in childhood may have developed a scarcity mentality that causes him to be stingy and ungenerous. The emptiness he experienced may also result in narcissistic tendencies, which are expressed in an insatiable need to be in the limelight or to be associated with a person or an organization that is in the limelight. Eventually others tire of his self-centered approach and no longer want to be around it.

- A person who was raised in an emotionally volatile and unpredictable environment develops a tendency toward fear and undue caution. Consequently, she refuses to take the kinds of risks that are necessary for spiritual journeying and soulful leadership.

It is impossible to overstate the exhaustion that results from all of this. But we need to remind ourselves that these are *unconscious, reflexive* responses to past realities and it is a work of God's grace if we are made aware of them—as painful as it may be. The more volatile and out of control our responses are, the more we can be sure that we are reacting out of old adaptive patterns rather than God-graced, Spirit-filled responses. While there may be dynamics in our current leadership situation that trigger such reflexive reactions, most often *our reactions* are more connected to the past than to what is actually going on in the present or what is called for in our current situation. Such reactions are not reflections of our true self in God—the person God created us to be and is creating us to be.

CONVERSION IN THE WILDERNESS

Moses discovered what we all must discover: that solitude is the place of our own conversion. In solitude we stop believing our own press. We discover that we are not as good as we thought but we are also more than we thought. As we slowly come in contact with our own dysfunctions, we unveil our need for security and all the ways we try to use God and others to get it. We are alarmed to discover that when the shepherd is starving, he or she may start devouring the sheep!

In solitude our illusions fall away and we see—sometimes with disturbing clarity—our competitiveness, our jealousies, our rage, our manipulations. We get in touch with our fears: fears of loneliness and abandonment, fears of really loving and allowing others to love us, fears of our sexuality and how powerful it is in combination with our spirituality. When we are in the company of others, it is easy to project our fears and negative feelings onto them; when we are in solitude, we must claim

> *Those things we cannot accept in ourselves*
>
> *we project upon others. If I do not admit my shadow side,*
>
> *I will unconsciously find another*
>
> *who will carry my shadow for me. Once this projection*
>
> *is made then I need not be upset with myself.*
>
> *My problems are now outside and I can fight them out there*
>
> *rather than within the real arena, myself.*
>
> JOHN ENGLISH, *SPIRITUAL PILGRIMS*

these inner experiences as our own. We discover that we are not who we thought we were in all of our self-aggrandizement, nor are we who other people think we are in all of their idealized projections.

If we stay in solitude long enough, we become safe enough with ourselves and with God to say, *Yes, this is who I am.* We are able to surrender to who we are—our limitations, our clinging and grasping and possessiveness, our selfishness and our fear. This is not a yes that says, *I will remain the same.* This is a yes that says to God, "I recognize what I am now, and I am none other than what I am. Whatever it is that most needs to be done in my life, you will have to do."

This is a very hard place for a leader to be. We are so used to being able to fix what needs fixing and push ahead with whatever needs doing that for a while we may find ways to try really, really hard to *do* something about what we are now seeing. Some of us will wear ourselves out trying to change ourselves before we realize that it is not about fixing; it is about letting go—letting go of old patterns that no longer serve us. This is frightening, because we are not sure such an approach will really work. And we are not sure what we might lose in the process. At this point it is helpful to remember that all we have to lose is what we don't really want anyway. All we stand to lose is the false self—the adaptive behaviors that are ultimately in opposition to the life of love and trust and being led by God that our hearts long for. To give ourselves to this process, we must trust that our true self is hidden with Christ in God, to be revealed as God sees that we are ready to live into it.

When we fail to name reality accurately, we are left to wander around in the wilderness of our illusions because we are hiding from ourselves and from God. We remain in bondage to that which does not take us forward in the life of grace, which is the very thing we say we want. The good news is that when we name our situation correctly—even (and perhaps most especially!) the parts that are so painful to acknowledge—we become more real. This is an awakening that leads to what is described in Christian tradition as the purgative way.

> The purgative way is a commitment to self-knowledge, which is essential preparation for serious Good News. Purgation (or self-simplification) is a way of "clearing the decks for action." The house is swept and polished and the garbage is collected and burned. The purpose of purgation is always remedial and never punitive. It is meant to help and not to punish. . . . The purgation of the soul provides an opportunity for growth and for the integration of the warring elements inside us.

Purgation leads to conversion, which is primarily about the "movement to a fully integrated and maturing life directed towards its true end and home." In that sense it is deeply hopeful. Conversion has to do with self-knowledge that brings with it an awareness of the discrepancy between what we are now and what we are meant to be. We may also discover with shock that even our "faith" has been, in part, enslaved to the ego. This awareness is accompanied by confession and repentance and maybe even a sense that we are falling apart. As the warm feelings associated with our earliest conversion experience are withdrawn, we are left with questions of the deepest kind. We long to be released from our own particular bondage, but we are also aware of our powerlessness to bring about this release.

I will never forget reflecting on these dynamics with a group of pastors while on retreat. After receiving teaching, they were released for a time of solitude to reflect on their own. When we rejoined one another, I asked them to tell us something of what had taken place in their time alone with God. One pastor blurted out, "I think *everything* I have done in ministry so far has been from my false self!"

My spontaneous response to his spontaneous outburst was to laugh—which is very unusual for me given such a sobering comment—but it was a laugh of sheer delight. Delight at seeing God at work in his life. Delight at his honesty. Delight in knowing that this is exactly the kind of self-awareness that opens us to new (and really good!) places on the spiritual journey—places of encounter with God that result in health, healing and greater authenticity in ministry.

> *The opportunity for conversion is brief,*
>
> *and our lives are littered with missed opportunities.*
>
> ALAN JONES, *SOUL MAKING*

INNER AND OUTER FREEDOM

These aspects of conversion along the purgative way are never meant to be harsh or punitive. Rather they are to facilitate a letting go that opens us to receive what we are being given. As we face who we are more honestly, we find we are finally ready for an encounter with God. The first leg of Moses' journey as a leader, then, was not to lead anyone else anywhere; it was to allow himself to be led into freedom from his own bondage. Before he could lead others into freedom, he needed to experience freedom himself. In solitude he was able to let go of the coping mechanisms that had served him well in the past but were completely inappropriate for the leader he was becoming. Yes, anger and the need to prove himself through the misuse of power would probably always be temptations for him (as we see in Numbers 20:1-13, for instance), but they would never again be his normal and accepted mode of operation. Now it was time to relinquish the weapons of false security, to come out of hiding and make room for something new to come.

Theophane, a Cistercian monk residing at St. Benedict's Monastery in Snowmass, Colorado, tells a striking story that beautifully illustrates such letting go:

> I saw a monk working alone in the vegetable garden. I squatted down beside him and said, "Brother, what is your dream?" He just looked straight at me. What a beautiful face he had.
>
> "I would like to become a monk," he answered.
>
> "But brother, you are a monk, aren't you?"
>
> "I've been here for 25 years, but I still carry a gun." He drew a revolver from the holster under his robe. It looked so strange, a monk carrying a gun.
>
> "And they won't—are you saying they won't let you become a monk until you give up your gun?"
>
> "No, it's not that. Most of them don't even know I have it, but I know."
>
> "Well then, why don't you give it up?"
>
> "I guess I've had it so long. I've been hurt a lot, and I've hurt a lot

of others. I don't think I would be comfortable without this gun."

"But you seem pretty uncomfortable with it."

"Yes, pretty uncomfortable, but I have my dream."

"Why don't you give me the gun?" I whispered. I was beginning to tremble.

He did, he gave it to me. His tears ran down to the ground and then he embraced me.

PUTTING DOWN THE GUN

Most of us have a gun—some way of protecting ourselves and making ourselves feel safe, hidden under the robe of our leadership persona. It is fairly easy to keep our gun hidden most of the time, but we know that it is there and that it is incongruent with the person God is calling us to be. We also know that if it were to "go off" unexpectedly, it would do great damage. We are uncomfortable living with it, but we are afraid to live without it. Sometimes we let ourselves dream of being free, of traveling without the need to pack a weapon. Holding on to our self-protective patterns is one manifestation of our unwillingness to surrender ourselves to God for the journey that is ahead.

But there is another desire that is greater than our desire to be safe. It is the desire to abandon ourselves to God and the life to which he is calling us. It is the desire to leave Egypt and journey with others to the Promised Land. Sometimes we hear God's whisper, "Why don't you give me the gun?" We feel ourselves trembling with longing and with pos-

---

The freedom question, then,

is not whether we can do whatever we want

but whether we can do what we most deeply want.

GERALD MAY, *THE AWAKENED HEART*

sibility, with fear and with hope. He waits quietly, patiently. And as we are ready, we give him that behavior, that pattern, that sin that we have relied on all these years, our tears running down to the ground. At least for a moment, we let ourselves feel what it's like to be free.

PRACTICE

Take a few moments at the close of this chapter to sit quietly in God's presence. Breathe deeply as way of loosening any tension you might be feeling or fear you might be holding. Allow yourself to "settle into" your humanity: your own history, your own personality, your own heritage, your own past and your own present. Without trying to fix anything or figure anything out, just let it be what it is and experience God's unconditional love for you and everything that has made you who you are.

After resting in God's presence, invite him to help you start seeing and naming the experiences that have shaped you. What are the patterns *underneath* the behaviors and situations that are disturbing to you at this time? Are there places in your life and leadership where you recognize that you are holding yourself tight rather than experiencing full surrender to God, where you recognize that you are not free? Are you aware of hidden patterns or even addictions that are hindering your spiritual journey and your effectiveness as a leader? *Do not* allow this time to degenerate into morbid introspection. *Do* invite God to guide the process and illuminate those areas that are important for you to see and name at this time. Remember that this part of Moses' journey took a very long time, so do not expect it all to come in a day or two.

■ ■ ■

O God, gather me
   to be with you
      as you are with me.
Keep me in touch with myself,

with my needs,
  my anxieties,
    my angers,
      my pains,
        my corruptions,
that I may claim them as my own
rather than blame them on someone else.

O Lord, deepen my wounds
  into wisdom;
shape my weaknesses
  into compassion;
gentle my envy
  into enjoyment,
    my fear into trust,
      my guilt into honesty.

O God, gather me
  to be with you
    as you are with me.

TED LODER, *GUERRILLAS OF GRACE*

4

THE PRACTICE OF PAYING ATTENTION

There the angle of the LORD

appeared to him in a flame of fire

out of a bush; he looked, and the bush

was blazing, yet it was not consumed.

Then Moses said, "I must turn aside

and look at this great sight."

EXODUS 3:2-3

It takes awhile to adjust to the truth one finally names in the wilderness. In fact it can leave one wandering around a little dazed. If I am not who I thought I was, then who am I? If I am letting go of the human reactivity that has driven my attempts at leadership up to this point, what will energize my leadership now? During this time we may experience serious doubt as to whether we are even cut out to be a leader. It might feel as if we are being dismantled.

God's word to us during such times is, *Be not dismayed. Even when you don't know who you are, I know who you are, and I will call to you when it is time.*

In the meantime, it is good to be wise with ourselves in the wake of this growing self-knowledge. Moses didn't rush to do anything radical or change everything all at once. Instead he stayed with a few things that he did know, the things that kept him grounded in the reality of his own life as it had been given to him. At least for the time being, he seemed content to keep doing what he had been doing—tending the flocks of his father-in-law, Jethro—without trying to grasp at anything or make anything happen. He had space to pay attention to his life as it had been given to him—the mundane and the miraculous. When we are taking time to pay attention, we never know when God will show up!

One day as Moses was carrying out a routine task—tending the flocks of Jethro—he ventured out a little farther than usual and came to Horeb, the mountain of God. It was almost as if God had been waiting for this moment—waiting for Moses to settle down and become real enough so he could address Moses directly. Up until this moment, God's presence in the story has been strongly implied, but no action or word has been directly attributed to him. But now that God had a real person to deal with, he could take a more direct approach!

It was an angel of the Lord that caused the initial commotion of the bush that was burning but not consumed. Because this was clearly beyond the normal, Moses turned aside to look. There seemed to be a cause-and-effect relationship between Moses' willingness to pay attention and God's willingness to speak. "When the LORD saw that he had turned aside to see, God called to him out of the bush" (Exodus 3:4). God spoke because Moses stopped, paused, noticed, turned aside!

TOO BUSY TO TURN ASIDE AND LOOK

I remember one season in my life when stopping to notice became almost impossible. At the time I was on staff at a church where, like most churches and organizations, we had lots of meetings. In fact, it was quite normal for our days to be so packed with back-to-back meetings that there was not time to take care of personal needs, let alone notice anything! On one such day when I had allowed myself to get scheduled in this manner, our youngest daughter, Haley, was at home sick. As I was headed into an afternoon meeting that would last until the end of the day, I realized that in the rush of things, I had not had a chance to call home and check on her. Since I could not be late for this meeting, the only thing I could do was call home while I was (quite literally) running through the hallways. It was not a pretty sight.

As I rounded a bend in one of those hallways—running, talking on the phone, skirt flapping in the breeze—I almost ran into another staff member coming down the hall from the opposite direction. He was so stunned by this mini-tornado careening down the hallway, and I was so embarrassed by the state I was in, that we both stopped and stared at each other with surprise. I finally mumbled a greeting and kept on going, all the while thinking, *When members of the pastoral staff are running down the hallways talking on their cell phones, there is something seriously wrong with this picture!*

I take full responsibility for my state of being on that day and most days. The way I was careening down that hallway was a microcosm of the whole, and it was no one's fault but my own. *I had allowed myself* to get scheduled in such a way that I was running from here to there with no time for listening and paying attention.

Many of us are choosing to live lives that do not set us up to pay attention, to notice those places where God is at work and to ask ourselves what these things mean. We long for a word from the Lord, but somehow we have been suckered into believing that the pace we keep is what leadership requires. We slide inexorably into a way of life that offers little or no opportunity for paying attention and then wonder why we are not hearing from God when we need God most.

There are times when a leader's deepest longing is to hear a word from the Lord. Beyond the muddle of all of our thoughts and ideas and brainstorming sessions, we long for an encounter with God that will penetrate all of that and bring some clarity to our situation. If we are aware of such a longing, a question we might ask ourselves is *How much paying attention am I doing—really? Do I have enough give in my schedule to be able turn aside and pay attention when there is something that warrants it? Could it be because I am moving so fast that I do not have time to turn aside and look? Do I even have mechanisms in my life that create space for paying attention, so that I don't miss the places where God himself is trying to communicate with me?*

I MUST TURN ASIDE AND LOOK AT THIS GREAT SIGHT

Contrast this mad dash through the hallways of our lives with Moses' experience of the burning bush. Solitude brought Moses to a place where he had slowed down enough to pay attention to the bush that was burning in the middle of his own life. At last, all other voices had quieted down enough that he could recognize a new Voice calling to him from this very unlikely place. Finally he was in a position to receive a word from the Lord.

The practice of "turning aside to look" is a spiritual discipline that by its very nature sets us up for an encounter with God. Elizabeth Dreyer, in her book *Earth Crammed with Heaven*, makes this provocative statement: "In a profound way, our intentionality is a key ingredient determining whether we notice God everywhere or only in church or only in suffering or nowhere. It all depends on how we choose to fashion our world."

These days there is such a glut of information and stimulation that it is often hard to know what to pay attention to. Should I take that class, read this highly recommended book, attend that conference, subscribe to this magazine or newsletter, interact with this blog or website, watch this television program, read this research, search the Internet just a little more . . . ? When we do create space where we can exercise some discretion about what to do with our time, we may find that we are spinning in circles from one worthy-of-attention thing to another, not knowing what to choose.

Learning to pay attention and knowing what to pay attention *to* is a key discipline for leaders but one that rarely comes naturally to those of us who are barreling through life with our eyes fixed on a goal. One of the downsides of visionary leadership is that we can get our sights set on something that is so far out in the future that we miss what's going on in our life as it exists now. We are blind to the bush that is burning in our own backyard and the wisdom that is contained within it. We squander the gift of this day just as it is, these people just they are, the uniqueness and the sweetness (even the bittersweetness) of this particular place on the journey just as it is, the voice of God calling to us in our own wilderness places.

Amid the welter of possible distractions, leaders need time in solitude so that we can notice those things we would otherwise miss due to the pace and complexity of our lives. We need moments in our life when we let the chaos settle a bit and invite God to show us evidence of his presence at work in big ways and subtle ways and allow him to guide us in our understanding of what these things mean. This practice alone can propel us into a very exciting part of the journey—a journey full of surprises and pronouncements and messages from God.

BURNING BUSHES
All of us have burning bushes in our lives, places that shimmer with

grace, alerting us to the possibility that God is at work doing something that we could not have predicted. As Elizabeth Barrett Browning wrote in her famous poem:

> Earth's crammed with heaven,
> and every common bush afire with God;
> but only he who sees, takes off his shoes—
>   the rest sit around it and pluck blackberries.

If spiritual leadership is anything. it is the capacity to see the bush burning in the middle of our own life and having enough sense to turn aside, take off our shoes and pay attention! The burning bush was, after all, a most ordinary object that became extraordinary because it was on fire with divine activity.

> *Spiritual leadership springs forth in grace*
>
> *from our very desire for God's presence.*
>
> *This does not take effort or striving. It takes courage,*
>
> *a kind of showing up, attentiveness.*
>
> GERALD MAY, LECTURE AT SHALEM INSTITUTE, MAY 1998

Recently our leadership community went on retreat to listen for God's direction regarding some fairly significant decisions facing the Transforming Center. We had spent a great deal of time taking an honest look at our financial picture and asking what it implied for smaller decisions and larger directional decisions. After getting the issues on the table and spending time in silence and personal reflection, we were not able to answer all of the larger, directional questions, but we did make some smaller decisions based on our financial forecast. One of those decisions was not to expand into additional office space that we had had our sights set on for quite some time. It was a painful but unanimous decision.

A few days later I explained our decision to those close to us, and that was that. Or so I thought.

Later on that day, one of the people who had heard about our decision sensed God saying, "You can help with that!" Having learned what the office space would cost, they sensed God's prompting to contribute the funds that would enable us to take the space for the year.

If I had been functioning primarily in the mentality of a typical board of directors, I probably would have seen the matter of office space as a closed issue, since we had already voted on it. I might have responded with appreciation to this person and tried to talk them into giving to support operational expenses or another agreed-upon line item. I might have assumed that since we didn't know everything about the organization's future, we should take a pass on this opportunity at this time. But instead I recognized the offer of this gift as a burning bush—something that was strange and unexpected and out of the ordinary. I could not have orchestrated it, and I knew that I needed to ask God what it meant rather than simply applying business logic to it.

As I paid attention to it in God's presence, what I heard was surprising and clarifying. First of all, I sensed God saying very clearly, "You don't know what your future holds, but I do, and I know what you will need for that future. That is why I am giving this to you." I even experienced a smile of anticipation about looking back at this moment from some future perspective and seeing more clearly why this office space was needed.

The second thing that God impressed upon me had to do with the nature of gifts. "What do you do with gifts?" I heard God ask.

"You receive them," I heard myself answer.

I heard God saying, "Stop your clinging and grasping. Just receive what I am giving you and then build your ministry with that."

What a simple and straightforward thing for God to say! There were many additional ramifications and applications to other areas of leadership, but suffice it to say that these two insights filled me with so much peace that there wasn't anything else I needed to know.

When I presented this new opportunity to our board, we agreed together that we would communicate honestly with our donor about the issues we were facing. If they still wanted to contribute for office expansion we would receive this gift from the hand of God. Beyond the particularities of the situation, a principle emerged that I knew would be significant for the next season of our life in ministry: we would move forward by building with what God gave us rather than straining and overreaching. This strengthened my soul profoundly and ushered me into a kind of rest in ministry that I had not experienced for a very long time. This particular burning bush served more than just the decision of that moment; it became a light that illuminated the path ahead.

BURNING HEARTS

Another way to stay in touch with the movement of God in our lives is to pay attention and give credence to that which burns within our own heart. The soulful leader trusts that in the midst of one's very public existence something is going on in the deep interior spaces of the soul that warrants serious attention.

In the New Testament story of the Emmaus road, the disciples' ability to listen to what was going on inside helped them recognize that the risen Christ was the one who had been with them as they traveled. This was a significant insight! Their willingness to pay attention to *what happened within them* as they interacted with the stranger on the road put them in touch with a dynamism that was qualitatively different from what they usually experienced. In the ordinary activity of sharing a meal, they took time to notice when an inner stirring signaled an encounter with Christ. "Were not our hearts burning within us while he was talking to us on the road?" they asked themselves as the evening deepened around them (Luke 24:32). The hope kindled within them after such a traumatic weekend of violence and death was immeasurable.

Moments such as these are there for all of us if we simply learn to notice—moments when our awareness opens up and we see something from a spiritual perspective that somehow changes everything. If we take time to pay attention, we see that God was with us—protecting us, guiding us, blessing us—and we realize how thin the veil really is between the material and spiritual worlds. We learn to recognize and respond to the spiritual reality that is all around us.

It is especially important for leaders to cultivate the ability to "discern the spirits" or "test the spirits to see whether they are from God" (see 1 Corinthians 12:10; 1 John 4:1). A leader who is committed to paying attention at this level develops a mature capacity for discernment that helps him or her distinguish the real from the phony, the true from the false, in the world "out there" but also in the interior world of thoughts and motives.

St. Ignatius of Loyola describes these inner dynamics as *consolation* and *desolation*. Consolation is the interior movement of the heart that gives a deep sense of life-giving connection with God, others and my most authentic self in God. It is the sense that all is right with the world, that I am free to be given over to God and to love even in moments of pain and crisis. Desolation is the loss of a sense of God's presence. I feel out of touch with God, with others and with my most authentic self. It is the experience of being off-center, full of turmoil, confusion and maybe even rebellion.

Experiences of consolation and desolation are not right or wrong; they just *are*. They need not be particularly momentous; in fact, they might seem relatively inconsequential until we learn to pay attention and listen for what they have to tell us. God's will for us is generally for us to do more of that which gives us life (John 10:10) and to turn away from those things that drain life from us and debilitate us.

Many of our smaller decisions and most of our significant decisions— even those decisions that require us to choose between two equally good options—involve the ability to notice what brings a sense of life and freedom (2 Corinthians 3:17) to our most authentic self in God. In Deuteronomy God instructed the whole company of Israel to pay attention in this way when he said, "I have set before you life and death, blessings and curses. Choose life so that you and your descendants may live." He wanted the Israelites to know that the wisdom that enables us to choose life is not something that we will find "out there," in heaven or across the ocean somewhere, but is very near to us—in our mouths and in our hearts for us to notice and observe (Deuteronomy 30:19-20). It is a visceral, in-the-body experience.

As we become more attuned to these subtle spiritual dynamics, we are able to distinguish between what is good (what moves us toward God and his calling on our life) and what is evil (what draws us away from God). In the experience I recounted earlier regarding the office space, I was flooded with a deep sense of consolation as we moved forward with the decision to receive the gift that had been offered. I still did not know all the reasons that God was giving it, but there was a compelling sense of peace and rightness about it. Every time I walked through the office space again, knowing that it would soon be ours, peace would flood me once again. If there had been desolation, I would have paid attention to that, too. I might not have wanted to, but I would have.

PAYING ATTENTION TO ALL THINGS BURNING

For a leader to take time to turn aside and look is no small thing. In the rush of normal life, we often blow right past the place where God is creating a stir to get our attention. But at the heart of spiritual leadership is the capacity to notice the activity of God so we can join him in it. Amid the welter of possible distractions, an essential discipline for leaders is to craft times of quiet in which we allow God to show us those things that we might otherwise miss. We need time for the chaos in our soul to settle so that we can turn aside to look at the great sights in our own life and seek understanding about what they mean.

This is also a practice leaders can carry out together. Recently, at an all-day board meeting, we decided to begin by paying attention to the burning bushes in our life together in ministry—those places where God's presence was clearly in evidence, where he was making himself known in surprising ways. We were coming into this particular meeting a bit discouraged; some of us were on edge with each other, and we weren't sure quite what to expect. This practice actually seemed a bit unnatural—given the mood we were in!—but we knew we needed some way of beginning that would set us on a positive path.

We started out by reflecting on the burning bush moment in Moses' life and then began listing things that we saw as burning bushes in our ministry. One was the gift of the office space and the enormous difference it was making in our ability to function efficiently. Another was the positive energy and momentum being generated by an innovative fundraiser that one of the board members had initiated. Our partnership with a like-minded organization was going very well, and we named some of the blessings associated with that. People were responding well to the published resources we were providing. We had recently established a ministry team and were sharing the ministry with others in a way that was very satisfying to us. Our finances were in good shape. The list seemed to go on, and pretty soon everyone was jumping in and naming evidences of God's activity among us.

As the list grew and each of us told stories about the difference our work was making in the lives of others, the tenor of the meeting became much more positive. By the end of the day, we were aware of a renewed sense of calling, we were convinced that God was with us, and we had a sense of direction regarding many of the issues on our agenda. The decisions we made that day were solid, not so much because we were smart but because they rested on noticing what God was doing among us and staying committed to the path that God's activity marked out for us.

One of the most soul-strengthening things that can happen to a leader in the crucible of ministry is to know that God is at work, to hear a Voice speaking that is not our own. Paying attention to all things burning in and around us keeps us in touch with what is truest about God, ourselves and our world so that we can hear God calling us by name again. The practice of paying attention awakens us to what is extraordinary in the midst of the ordinary. As we live our lives in humble response to the One who is calling to us out of the burning bush in our own lives, we discover that we are standing on holy ground more often than we think.

PRACTICE

Begin your time in quiet today with the intention to begin cultivating solitude as a place for paying attention. First, pay attention to your breathing. Notice how in the rush of things your breathing can tend to be shallow and something you take for granted. On this day, take time to breathe deeply and slowly. Receive each breath as God's gift to you, evidence that he wants you to be alive today.

Now take some time to pay attention to your life over the last days or even weeks. First of all, notice any way that focusing too much on "the vision" might be hampering your ability to receive the present moment and the gifts it brings. Don't throw out your vision, but take some time to pay attention to your life *as it is being given to you right now.* Be very specific about naming the gifts in it and be grateful.

Then, notice anything that is external to you that may be surprising and out of the ordinary. It doesn't matter whether it feels significant or insignificant; the fact that God is bringing it to your attention and speaking to you about it is reason enough to take off your shoes and respond with reverence. As God reveals something in your life that may be a burning bush, take time to ponder what it might mean, with utter willingness to follow the wisdom or guidance that comes.

Also, notice your own inner dynamics. Notice any point when your heart has burned within you in the midst of your day-to-day life. Give yourself time and space to ponder its spiritual significance. Without judging or evaluating or calling anything right or wrong, notice times of consolation and desolation that you have ignored in the rush of things. Listen for God's invitation for you to *choose life*—even in relation to leadership decisions you face. Allow the dynamics of consolation and desolation to speak to whatever decisions you are facing. Remember, you are allowed to choose life.

■　■　■

O God,
let something essential and joyful happen in me now,
something like the blooming of hope and faith,
　like a grateful heart,
　　like a surge of awareness
　　　of how precious each moment is,
that now, not next time,
now is the occasion
　to take off my shoes,
　　to see every bush afire,
　　　to leap and whirl with neighbor,
　　　　to gulp the air as sweet wine
until I've drunk enough
　to dare to speak the tender word:
　　"Thank you";
　　　"I love you";
　　　　"You're beautiful";
　　　　　"Let's live forever beginning now";
　　　　　　And "I'm a fool for Christ's sake."

TED LODER, *GUERRILLAS OF GRACE*

5

The Conundrum
of Calling

When the LORD saw that he had

turned aside to see, God called

to him out of the bush.

EXODUS 3:4

When God was sure that he had Moses' undivided attention, the first thing he talked to him about was his calling. Finally the true God was able to address the real Moses.

In our day it is easy to dismiss the idea of calling as a mere concept, but God called to Moses, out of the burning bush saying (in effect), "I know the question about your identity has been a little confusing for you, but I have always known who you are. You are a Hebrew. No matter where you live, no matter who raised you, no matter how anyone tries to beat it out of you, no one can take that away from you. You know what it is to be displaced. You know what it is to live your life on someone else's terms, to see the injustice of it all and want to do something about it. In the very essence of your being, you are someone who is not willing to let injustice go unanswered; your care for your people and their well-being is deep and genuine. Now that *you* know who you are, I am calling you to *do* something out of the essence of your being. You have submitted to the rigors of the wilderness. *Come now, and I will send you to Pharaoh, so that you may bring my people, the sons of Israel, out of Egypt. "*

If Moses was paying attention at all, this was likely a moment when everything started to make sense. It was becoming clear that his calling was inextricably interwoven with his human situation and his personal history. His passion for his people and the strong sense of justice that had caused his violent outburst back in Egypt lay at the heart of what God was now asking him to do. Even though his violent reaction to the injustice that he witnessed had been terribly wrong, the incident itself was not irrelevant. It arose from something real within him.

Back then he had been propelled primarily by his own raw, human anger. But being angry is not the same thing as being called. *Now* something new was starting to unfold. Now God was *calling* him to move beyond undisciplined, angry outbursts to a more substantive and helpful response. Now God was guiding him to embrace more fully the person he had always been and, paradoxically, to also transcend it!

Beyond just naming what was false within him, God was calling for Moses' true self to come out of hiding; God was calling him to claim his full identity and to lead boldly from that place. It was a lot to ask, but now—forty years later!—Moses' moment had come. The time for hiding out in the wilderness was almost over. God was asking him to step up and be everything he was and everything God would call him to be, for the good of many. Our transformation is never for ourselves alone. It is always for the sake of others.

HOLY GROUND

When God calls, it is a very big deal. It is holy ground. It produces within us such reverence and awe that it is hard to know what to do with ourselves. Finally the whole of our life begins to make sense, and new awareness of the divine orchestration that has brought us to this moment makes us want to take off our shoes or fall on our face or maybe even argue with God about the improbability of it all. But no matter how much we may want to resist, the landscape of our life has opened up. Every single thing that didn't make sense when it happened, that seemed too harsh or too random or too shameful, now finds its place in the storyline that brought us here.

We "see" with new eyes that God's call on our life is so tightly woven into the fabric of our being, so core to who we are, that to ignore it or to refuse it would be to jeopardize our well-being. If we were to try to compromise or to live it only halfway, we'd run the risk of plunging into emptiness and meaninglessness. Jonah tried to walk away from his calling but ended up in the belly of a fish. Jeremiah tried to walk away from his call to be a prophet, but it was like a fire shut up in his bones and he soon became weary of holding it in.

Harvard Business School professor and former CEO of Medtronics Bill George has written a marvelous book on leadership called *True North* which is based on in-depth research and interviews of 125 of today's top leaders. Virtually all the leaders interviewed for his book found their passion to lead through the uniqueness of their life story. "When asked what motivates them to lead, authentic leaders say they find their motivation through understanding their own stories. Their stories enable them to know who they are and to stay focused on their True North." Starbucks founder Howard Schultz is a case in point.

When Schultz was only seven years old, his father had a work-related accident in which he broke his ankle. As a result, he lost his job and the family's health benefits. Workers' compensation did not yet exist, and Schultz's mother could not work because she was seven months pregnant. Their family life deteriorated quickly, and the memories of how this situation broke his father's spirit motivated Howard to incorporate access to health coverage for qualified employees who work as few as twenty hours a week as a foundational value of the company. This is the story behind the story.

Today Starbucks is known as an excellent place to work, and one of the biggest reasons is this deeply held value of caring for the needs of its employees. Schultz says, "My inspiration comes from seeing my father broken from the thirty terrible blue-collar jobs he had over his life, where an uneducated person just did not have a shot. . . . I wanted to build the kind of company my father never had a chance to work for, where you would be valued and respected, no matter where you came from. . . . Offering health care was a transforming event in the equity of the Starbucks brand that created unbelievable trust with our people."

Clearly, Schultz's calling is more than just providing customers with a good cup of coffee. As he came to terms with his own life story and reframed his image of his dad, he moved beyond seeing his father as a failure and came to believe that the system had crushed him. "After he died, I realized I had judged him unfairly. He never had the opportunity to find fulfillment and dignity from meaningful work." One of the results of connecting his leadership with his life story was that Schultz channeled his drive into building a company where his father would have been proud to work.

A SPIRITUALITY OF CALLING

The soul of leadership begins with who we are—really. Not who we think we are, not who we would like to be, not who others believe us to be. God's call includes (yet is not limited to) the particularities of our life, our heritage, our personality, our foibles, our passions and deepest orientation, and even our current life situation. Being called by God is one of the most essentially *spiritual* experiences of human existence, because it is a place where God's presence intersects with a human life. Our calling emerges from who we really are—in all the rawness and sinfulness of it as well as in all the glory and God-givenness of it.

> *Vocation does not come from willfulness.*
>
> *It comes from listening. I must listen to my life*
>
> *and try to understand what it is truly about—*
>
> *quite apart from what I would like it to be about—*
>
> *or my life will never represent anything real*
>
> *in the world, no matter how earnest my intentions.*
>
> PARKER PALMER, *LET YOUR LIFE SPEAK*

There is no escaping who we are. Leadership will not help us escape ourselves—it will only bring who we are into bolder relief! Leadership calls us to deepen our willingness to become more than what we are right now so that we can say yes to that which is ours to do. "Vocation at its deepest level is, 'This is something I can't not do, for reasons I am unable to explain to anyone else and don't fully understand myself but that are nonetheless compelling.'"

Before calling has anything to do with *doing,* it has everything to do with *being* that essence of yourself that God knew before the foundations of the earth, that God called into being and that God alone truly knows. It is the call to be who we are and at the same time to become more than we can yet envision.

God called Moses to be who he was, but he was also calling him to *become something that he was not yet*—a leader who would bring God's people out of bondage. Moses did not yet see himself as the kind of leader God knew him to be. It is possible that he thought of himself more as a man of action than as someone with the kind of verbal prowess and persuasiveness that this particular calling would require. In fact, he had a few things he needed to say to God about it, and what follows in Exodus 3 is an amazing conversation in which Moses pushes God to the limit with his questions and objections. But God does not back down, because calling is first and foremost the calling to be yourself, that self that God created you to be.

Our calling is woven into the very fabric of our being *as we have been created by God,* and it encompasses everything that makes us who we are: our genetics, innate orientations and capacities, our personality, heredity and life-shaping experiences, and the time and place into which we were born. "Vocation does not come from a voice 'out there' calling me to be something I am not. It comes from a voice 'in here' calling me to be the person I was born to be, to fulfill the original selfhood given to me at birth by God."

But this is not as easy as it sounds. By the time we even know that there is such a thing as a true or authentic self, the false self has already taken over to the extent that it is hard to tell what is false and what is true. Over time a great gulf has developed between who we really are and the designs and plans that the ego has for us. It can be a very complicated matter to untangle all the threads.

But if we are willing to pay attention, we can catch glimpses of the true self by noticing what brings deep gladness and a sense of meaning to our existence. Some of the best hints about who we really are come from memories of unguarded moments in childhood and youth, moments when we were caught up in the essence of being rather than driven by self-conscious doing and performing. If we are able to look back on our childhood self with curiosity and attention, we may remember moments when we were completely and unreservedly ourselves and wonder what those mean for us today:

- A little boy loses himself for hours taking things apart and putting them back together.

- With great care, a little girl crafts three-point sermons for family devotions and delivers them with innocence and pride.

- A little boy routinely slips away from the noise of family life and spends hours lying in the grass and looking up at the sky, dreaming up stories and scenarios that might later become realities.

- A little girl puts on puppet shows and plays for family and friends.

- A little boy is fascinated with color and texture and is endlessly combining them with pencils, paints and Play-Doh.

- A little girl plays soccer and hockey and football with the boys before she learns that usually it doesn't work that way.

These unselfconscious proclivities are expressions of the essential self that God knew and called into being before there was anything else we thought we needed to be. This essential self existed before we had anything to prove, before we had any sense of what was socially acceptable or useful, before we needed to figure out how to make a living. And it is real. Just as real as, if not more so than, the wounds and the adaptive patterns that we have come to identify with.

It can be sobering to realize how easily our connection with what is most true about us can get lost in the context of leadership. There are times when calling involves finding our way *back to* what is real so that we can bring more of who we really are into the present.

BEYOND CAREER DEVELOPMENT

In our day it may seem almost archaic to talk about the idea of calling. Tilden Edwards wisely observes, "Calling is a much abused word today. In the church it can be little more than a pious euphemism for doing what we feel like doing. Such abuse is brought to celebration in the secular culture, when doing what we feel like doing, attained by any way we feel like doing it, seems often to be what lies behind 'career development.'"

However, the biblical idea of calling is not easily dismissed. Its meaning is richly layered. In its simplest and most straightforward meaning, the verb *to call* refers to the capacity living creatures have to call out to one another, to stay connected, to communicate something of importance. Even at this most basic level the dynamic of calling is profound, because it reminds us that calling is first of all highly relational: it has to do with one being (God) reaching out and establishing connection with another (us). It is an interpersonal connection and communication that is initiated by God and thus demands our attention and our response even as a basic courtesy.

In the Old Testament, the idea of calling goes beyond this most basic meaning to include the idea of naming and calling something *into being*. In his book *The Call,* Os Guinness writes, "Such decisive, creative naming is a form of making. . . . Calling is not only a matter of being and doing what we are but also of becoming what we are not yet but are called by God to be."

In the New Testament, the idea of calling is almost synonymous with salvation and the life of faith itself. We are saved from being who we are not and called to be who we are. God calls us first and foremost to belong to him, but our secondary calling is to answer God's personal address to us. It is to say yes to his summons to serve him in a particular way at a particular point in history. To say yes to our calling is one more step in the journey of faith which involves a glad, joyful self-surrender. It is living in the awareness that the most wonderful thing in the world is to be completely given over to a loving God.

ARGUING IT OUT WITH GOD

Even so, Moses tried his best to argue his way out of his calling, and interestingly enough, most of his questions and objections had to do with identity issues and the lack of a sense of self that continued to plague him: Who am I? Who are you? What if they won't listen to me or believe me? What if I'm not good enough? What will I say?

Moses' unhealthy patterns—particularly his confusion about his identity and his inability to clearly define himself in relation to others—showed up most fully here, in his interactions with God! These patterns were so deeply ingrained that he was living them out even in his most private moments with God. This is what we all do. We all bring the relating patterns that we have learned in relationships with other human beings into our relationship with God. And it is here that these patterns must be undone.

It is not unusual for us to feel the kind of resistance or ambivalence that Moses felt in the face of God's call even as our heart is leaping with the awareness that God is at work in our life. Any kind of authentic calling usually takes us to a place where we have serious objections of some sort, places where we feel inadequate—where we confront our own willfulness and our preconceived ideas about how we thought our life would go, where we think what God is asking us to do is downright impossible or where we just don't want to take the risk. But one of the ways we recognize calling is that it has come about in ways that could not be humanly orchestrated and so it cannot be easily dismissed. "Vocational calling involves more riskiness and uncertainty. While you won't be given 'more than you can bear,' you will be led by 'a way you do not know' to be a channel for grace in ways you cannot adequately predict."

But God answers all of Moses' objections (and ours!) with variations on a single theme—the promise of God's presence in the crucible of leadership.

When Moses asked, "Who am I to even think of doing such a thing?" God's answer was "I will be with you" (see Exodus 3:11-12).

When Moses asked how the Hebrews would know it was God who

sent him, God's answer was "Thus you shall say to the Israelites, 'I AM has sent me to you.'" God went on to promise that Moses would be empowered to perform wonders that would prove he had been in God's presence (3:13—4:9).

When Moses asked, "What if they won't believe me?" God's answer was to give him more signs (4:1-9).

When Moses mentioned his feelings of inadequacy, God said, "Who gave you your capacity for speech in the first place? Who made your mouth? I will be with your mouth and teach you what to say" (see 4:10-12).

The answer to all of Moses' concerns about why anyone would follow him was simple: *The people will follow you because you have met me. Because you know my name deep in your being. That is what qualifies you to be a spiritual leader, and that is why people will be willing to follow you right out of the place they have known for so long to a place that is brand-new.*

In this amazing dialogue Moses experienced the great paradox of calling: God was saying, in essence, it is all about you (because you are the one I have called) and it's not about you at all (because it was all about me and my work in and through you). And all God's promises to him were fulfilled. When the children of Israel saw what God accomplished for them through Moses' leadership, they believed in God and they believed in his servant Moses.

Solitude, then, is that place where we fight it out with God if we need to—all the way down to the mat. Leadership, even at its best, is terribly demanding, and it is crucial that we argue out our ambivalence about our calling to leadership openly with God so that it doesn't leak out and create uncertainty in those we are serving.

Most of us, at one point or another, experience profound questions about what it is we are leading or some aspect of it. One of the aspects of my own calling that I have had to wrestle with in recent years has to do with the challenges of leading a not-for-profit organization. Never in my wildest dreams had I planned to lead a not-for-profit organization that was not a church. I will admit that I have argued with God quite a bit about this one. At times I have grown tired of carrying the weight of being the "buck stops here" person. On more than one occasion I have spent time in solitude wrestling with God—trying to come to peace with my calling so that I could get on with the business of leading and so that my ambivalence would not confuse those I was leading. Many pastors come to the point of questioning their call to the pastorate and moving on to something else. Ministry is always much harder than we think.

Jesus himself used his solitude in the Garden of Gethsemane to wrestle with God about whether there was another way for him to fulfill his calling than the hard road of the cross. All of his life he had known what he was on earth to do, but when it was time to walk all the way into it, he had a few things he needed to say to God about it. He stayed in that garden until he knew for sure that this was God's way for him—until he had really come to terms with it—and then he emerged to walk the path that was laid out for him. Perhaps this kind of passage is characteristic of all true calls. There is a difference between knowing your path and walking your path.

THE FATAL QUESTION

At the heart of it, Moses' story is one of calling. Why else would one choose to leave security and wealth, power and influence for such a risky proposition? After the initial excitement, leading his people was just plain hard all the time. There was very little glory and there were many small humiliations. But there were also encounters with God that were profoundly *dis*orienting and *re*orienting.

Ezekiel had a similar experience of calling: "[The LORD] said to me: O mortal, stand up on your feet, and I will speak with you. And when he spoke to me, a spirit entered into me and set me on my feet. . . . He said to me, Mortal, I am sending you to the people of Israel, to a nation of rebels who have rebelled against me" (Ezekiel 2:1-3). Ezekiel's story mirrors Moses' in that it demonstrates that *the call of God comes to us as mortals*. It comes to us in the place where we are most human, and it is the Spirit of God who comes over us to empower our human frailty so that we can even hear the call, let alone answer it.

Somehow we know that this moment is different. This is not about making a brilliant career move. It is not about security. It is not about success or failure or anything else the ego wants for us. It is not about choosing among several attractive options. This is about the Spirit of God setting us on our feet and telling us, "This is yours to do. Whether they hear or refuse to hear, whether it feels to you as if you are failing or succeeding, you are to speak my words."

The great psychologist Carl Jung once made this observation: "To the extent that a man is untrue to the law of his being and does not rise to personality, he has failed to realize his life's meaning. Fortunately, in her kindness and patience, Nature never puts the fatal question as to the meaning of their lives into the mouths of most people. And where no one asks, no one need answer."

I'm not sure Moses was asking or wondering about such things when he was wandering around with his sheep in the wilderness. In fact, it seems that Moses had gotten quite comfortable with his wilderness existence, but the fatal question of the meaning of his life got put to him anyway. When God spoke to him out of the burning bush, he was asking Moses to take the difficult journey of "rising to personality"—rising to the full purpose of his being here on earth—in order to realize the meaning of his life. He was asking him to become more fully the person he had always been and at the same time to transcend it.

Some people seem to make it through life without ever having to wrestle with the fatal question. They seem to move through life with ease—making a living, enjoying the fruits of their labor, taking what seems to be an easy or at least a rather clearly marked path to security and success—while others seem to be called to make commitments that require us to do strange things and orient our lives toward realities that others do not even see. It is hard to be this kind of person—to have a fire burning within us that we can't "shut up in our bones" without doing damage to the soul. It's hard to keep answering a calling that continually takes us right out to the edge of our faith and our human limitations. Sometimes we are tempted to feel resentful.

But a true leader is one who *has* heard the fatal question. This is a person who has seen a vision of what could be and who continues to take steps in that direction against all odds. We might argue with God a bit. We might put forth every excuse that comes to mind. But God always wins this argument, because every time we go deep inside to listen, we know that what God is calling us to do is ours to do and that the path before us is ours to walk. We know it is the meaning of our life. And so we say yes. For better and for worse, we say yes to meaning. We say yes to God.

> *Calls are essentially questions. They aren't questions*
>
> *you necessarily need to answer outright;*
>
> *they are questions to which you need to respond,*
>
> *expose yourself, and kneel before. You don't want an*
>
> *answer you can put in a box and set on a shelf.*
>
> *You want a question that will become a chariot*
>
> *to carry you across the breadth of your life.*
>
> GREGG LEVOY, *CALLINGS*

PRACTICE

In the quietness, allow yourself to remember the time when you first began to sense God's call on your life. Maybe it was a moment like Moses' when you heard God speak deep into your heart with great clarity, or perhaps your sense of calling grew in strength and conviction over time.

Remember where you were, what it sounded like, what it felt like, what you said to God, how you resisted and how you said yes.

After taking time to be with that initial experience, ask, *What is God saying to me these days about my calling? As I settle into myself more fully, what am I learning about my calling? Is there any place where I am resisting who I am or have lost touch with who I am? Where am I still wrestling with God and needing assurance of his presence with me? Am I willing to say yes again?*

■　■　■

I believe in all that has never yet been spoken.
I want to free what waits within me
so that what no one has dared to wish for

may for once spring clear
without my contriving.
If this is arrogant, God, forgive me,
but this is what I need to say.
May what I do flow from me like a river,
no forcing and no holding back,
the way it is with children.

Then in these swelling and ebbing currents,
these deepening tides moving out, returning,
I will sing you as no one ever has,

streaming through widening channels
into the open sea.

RAINER MARIA RILKE, *RILKE'S BOOK OF HOURS*

6

GUIDING OTHERS
ON THE SPIRITUAL
JOURNEY

From the wilderness of Sin
the whole congregation of the
Israelites journeyed by stages,
as the LORD commanded.

EXODUS 17:1

The best guide for any journey is one who has made the journey him- or herself—perhaps multiple times—and thus knows something about the terrain, the climate, the beauties, dangers and challenges present at each point along the way. Part of what qualified Moses to lead the people of Israel out of their bondage was that he had already been on his own journey out of bondage and into the freedom to follow God fully.

By the time God called Moses to lead the Israelites out of Egypt, he had already taken his own journey in the wilderness. He had traversed the wilderness territory of his own soul for forty years, and he knew how to find God there. He had learned how to listen and then follow God's word to him. Moses' faithfulness to his own spiritual journey was the best possible preparation for leading the Israelites out of their long bondage and into the freedom that God had for them.

> *The great illusion of leadership is to think that man*
> *can be led out of the desert by someone*
> *who has never been there.*
>
> HENRI NOUWEN, *THE WOUNDED HEALER*

The exodus is a great metaphor for the spiritual journey—the journey from spiritual bondage to freedom in Christ that we take as individuals and also together as the people of God. It can be seen as a metaphor for the whole journey from salvation to finding our true home in heaven. But it can also be a metaphor for a time when God is calling us to greater freedom in a particular area of our life or a time when God is calling us to leave familiar territory behind so that we can enter into something new. The places through which the Israelites passed on their journey serve well in helping us understand the stages of our own journey.

These stages do not represent a linear journey where we arrive at some location and then we're done. Rather, they represent a cyclical process that continues to move us in the direction of greater spiritual maturity and greater freedom and abandonment to God. This process will not be complete until we reach our final destination of eternity spent in the presence of God. It is one thing to inspire people to visions of what the Promised Land is like; it is quite another to understand the stages of the journey between here and there so that we can guide folks through them and actually arrive at our destination.

Understanding the stages that we have passed through on our own journey is excellent preparation for leading others on the journey with gentleness and skill. An understanding of stages can help us instill confidence and provide reassurance during those parts of the journey that are challenging and difficult. Part of Moses' role as a leader was to lead the Israelites in each stage of their physical journey at the Lord's command. "These are the stages by which the Israelites went out of the land of Egypt . . . under the leadership of Moses and Aaron. Moses wrote down their starting points, stage by stage, by command of the LORD; and these are their stages according to their starting places" (Numbers 33:1-2).

Many of the places the Israelites passed through on their physical journey correspond to passages in the spiritual journey. Being able to recognize the markers along the way can help us provide guidance for this journey we have embarked upon with those we are leading. What follows is a description of the stages Moses led his people through, by God's grace, with application to the spiritual journey as we experience it today.

PREAWARENESS

The first stage in the spiritual journey is *preawareness*. This is the time when, like the Israelites, we are not even aware that we are in bondage or that we need God to lead us into something more. There may even be good things going on ("the Israelites were fruitful and prolific," Exodus 1:7), and we are lulled into believing that this is as good as it gets. At this stage our way of life seems to be working pretty well, and we assume that this is the way everyone lives. This is the non-Christian person before they are even aware that they are seeking anything. This is the person or congregation that has been on the Christian path for a long time and yet now is having a sense that there must be something more. It is when we are on the verge of seeing a sin pattern or a part of the false self that we aren't quite ready to name because we know that it will rock the boat of life as we know it.

In God's time God begins to move us toward a new level of awareness. We might get an inkling that something is not quite right—a question bubbles up, a longing stirs, we spend time with someone who seems more free, more attractive, more healthy or whole. We have a vague sense of dis-ease, but for the most part we are able to keep it outside our awareness. The preawareness stage can go on for a long time, because there is something comforting and secure about life as we know it. Because we are not ready to move into the unknown, we find ways to maintain the status quo, and in so doing, we abdicate responsibility for dealing with the issues of our life. Like that of the Israelites, our bondage is familiar. It is a way of life that makes sense to us given the level of understanding we currently have.

AWARENESS

Eventually something happens that heightens our *awareness* that our heart is longing for something more. We realize that we are not completely free, and we begin to at least open up to the possibility of moving in a new direction. This could be a single event or an accumulation of events that we can no longer dismiss or ignore.

For the Israelites, it was increasing oppression by both a king who did not know Joseph and the taskmasters who were carrying out his orders. This oppression was motivated by fear, as all oppression is. The

Egyptian pharaoh was afraid that the children of Israel would become strong, fight against Egypt and eventually escape. The king became so frightened of the potential power of these lively people that he ordered all the baby boys to be killed at birth. As the ruthlessness of the taskmasters increased and the bitterness of their lives became unbearable, the Israelites groaned under the conditions of their slavery. It was no longer possible to pretend that everything was as it should be.

At the same time God was already starting to prepare a leader to lead them out of bondage. Even before they were aware that they were in bondage, God was beginning to put the necessary components in place so that when the time was right they would take their first steps toward freedom with the support and the guidance they needed. Meanwhile Moses was going through his own process of struggling with awareness and trying to figure out what to do. Their journeys were running parallel with each other's even though they were not knowingly connected yet in any way. It was painful for Moses to see what he was seeing, but his initial attempt to do something about it had failed so miserably that he had run away and tried to hide. Not only was he running away from having his sin found out, but he was also running away from the responsibility that increased awareness inevitably brings. Out of sight, out of mind.

That's the way it is for all of us. We might try to ignore what we've seen and hide from the responsibility that goes along with it, but if we want to get on with the spiritual journey, we must look at reality full in the face. Denial is a lot less painful than awareness, but if we remain in denial, we are left stuck in our bondage. In the awareness (or awakening) stage we wake up; we are willing to see and to name truth more accurately. Leadership at this stage requires helping people have the courage to name reality and keep facing into it. In a congregation it might be the reality that people aren't growing. Or that the young people are leaving the church. Or that our pace of life is not working and we as leaders are longing for more. In an organization, it might be that we have gotten away from our mission, or that our mission no longer captures our sense of what we are called to do. Or that we have slipped into patterns of working or relating that are no longer life giving. Or it could be helping individuals keep facing what is true in their own lives and taking responsibility for how that is impacting our life together.

Awareness always calls us to take responsibility for responding to what we are seeing—which is another reason that many of us seek to avoid awareness for as long as we can. But when the pain of staying the same is greater than the pain of changing, we are ripe for making a move. The emotions that we feel in response to what we have seen might be volatile during this time, but they serve a good purpose—they give us the energy and resolve to begin preparing to move in a new direction.

Awareness also involves being able to see the possibility of living in a new way, and oftentimes it takes a visionary leader or at least someone who is a little bit further down the road to help us see what we have not yet been able to see. Another function of leadership is to help people get in touch with their longings and see the possibility of a new way. In the midst of the Israelites' growing awareness that they could not go on as they were, Moses and Aaron arrived on the scene to assure them that God had seen their misery and would empower them to leave Egypt and change their lives. In the awareness stage, all of us need those who will help us see what is real about our current situation, but we also need someone who can assure us that there is another way and that it is possible for us to move in that direction—as risky as it might seem.

TURNING POINT
So the Israelites began to let themselves dream of the freedom to live together in a community that is free to worship and serve God freely. Martin Luther King Jr. let himself see a world in which black children and white children live together in equality without the clouds of segregation hanging over their heads. A person who becomes aware of how

the pain of their past has twisted their relational patterns begins to en-vision what it would be like to face into the pain and come to a place of greater freedom on the other side. A person who has resisted surrender to God begins to envision what it would be like to say yes to the spiritual journey. A person who has lived their entire life according to oughts and shoulds imposed on them by others begins to get a glimpse of what it would be like to live out of a truer self that has been called by God. A *turning point* has been reached.

But things often get worse before they get better. While the Israelites' awareness was growing, the circumstances causing their suffering got worse. Now they were required to make bricks without straw, and when they weren't able to keep up with their quotas, they were beaten even more brutally. The deterioration of our situation might seem like an un-necessary piece of the journey, but it is actually an important part of the process because *it brings us to a turning point* where we are willing to *do* something about our situation. This is the straw that breaks the camel's back. This is that last thing that puts it over the edge for us, and after this, nothing can be the same. Before this we were waffling—tossed back and forth between the awareness of our bondage and the awareness of all we have to lose if we get up and make a needed change.

At this point, things can get pretty messy and chaotic. Like the Israel-ites, we might find it hard to listen to the voice of hope "because of [our] broken spirit and [our] cruel slavery" (see Exodus 6:9). This is a very chal-lenging time for the leader, too, as he or she realizes that things are not go-ing to be quite as easy as we had hoped. In Moses' case, the people were no longer listening to him, and he took it personally. It confirmed his worst fears about being a poor and ineffective speaker. He even had an "I told you so" moment with God: "The Israelites have not listened to me; how then shall Pharaoh listen to me, poor speaker that I am?" (Exodus 6:12).

But all of this was the darkness before the dawn. This is God's mo-ment to come through—and he does!—with signs and wonders that will free us for the journey that is ahead.

> *It is good to be between a ruined house of bondage*
>
> *and a holy promised land.*
>
> LEONARD COHEN

THE ROUNDABOUT WAY

And they're off! The signs and wonders that God performs through Moses and Aaron along with the plagues have done their good work, and the Egyptians are happy to see the Israelites go. In the midst of much hoopla and celebration, they embark on an incredible journey.

Their newfound freedom is really exciting at first. A deeper spiritual journey is, after all, what we have been longing for, and actually getting on the way is quite the emotional high. The victories that have brought us to this point may even leave us with a sense that we are somewhat invincible (nothing's gonna stop us now!) and we are ready for anything. After the stress of decision-making and change, we are ushered into a time of spiritual flourishing, characterized by great enthusiasm, gratitude, voracious learning and service.

God in his kindness leads us in such a way that at this stage we don't face challenges that are more than we can handle. God intentionally led the Israelites by "the roundabout way" rather than the most direct route, because God knew that they weren't ready to take on the challenges that a more direct route would have brought: "When Pharaoh let the people go, God did not lead them by way of the land of the Philistines, although that was nearer; for God thought, 'If the people face war, they may change their minds and return to Egypt.' So God led the people by the roundabout way of the wilderness" (Exodus 13:17-18). Even though they might have preferred a more direct route to their dream, it was actually a great kindness that God prevented them from encountering more than they were ready to handle.

The *roundabout way* may not be the most direct route, but it represents a wonderful era in the spiritual life when God shows up in very tangible ways that assure us of his presence on the journey. Like the cloud by day and the pillar of fire by night, visible signs of God's presence are never far away. In the Israelites' case, the presence of God mediated through these symbols never left its place in front of the people, because the main purpose of this season was to protect them from challenges they were not ready to face and to teach them through experience day after day that the presence of God would never leave them.

During this time we settle into a period of normalcy when we learn what it is to live freely in the presence of God and to rely on that presence for our sustenance. The ability to rely on God that is being developed during this time is foundational to the spiritual life and will serve us well when the first challenge hits and we enter into "the great and terrible wilderness" (Deuteronomy 8:15).

Although we may feel invincible (based on our earlier triumphs), God knows that we are not. He knows that if we were to experience any real dangers, toils and snares, we wouldn't be ready for them. One of the main lessons we learn during this stage of the spiritual journey is that God is not in any particular hurry to get us to the Promised Land. He is much more concerned about the transforming work he is doing *in us* to prepare us for greater responsibilities of freedom living. Onlookers may observe our journey and, like Pharaoh, think we are just wandering around aimlessly, but God knows what he is doing; he is concerned about strengthening our faith so that we are prepared when there are real challenges to be faced.

TIMES OF TESTING

And the challenges do come. Somewhere along this way, we are faced with our first real *obstacle*. It is usually quite unexpected, and we are not prepared. For the Israelites, their first obstacle was the Red Sea. We all know the story: as they approached what appeared to be an uncrossable sea, they looked back only to find that the Egyptians had changed their minds and were pursuing them to take them back into slavery. Even with all that they had experienced of God's presence with them, their faith faltered. For the first time, they experienced real ambivalence about this journey toward freedom and what it was now requiring of them. They attacked Moses and accused him of bringing them out to the wilderness to die. They were convinced that God had abandoned them, and they longed to go back to Egypt where at least there was a bit more security.

This ambivalence about the rigors of the spiritual journey is a predictable part of any true journey, and it is helpful for us as leaders to know this so that we don't take it too personally. A wise leader can help people understand their ambivalence as a very normal response to the challenges of the journey rather than an excuse to run back to what feels more secure.

It is important to realize that the people's reaction had very little to do with Moses. Their reaction was more about where they were on the journey and what God was doing in them and in the Egyptians through this challenge. While we should be hesitant to say that God causes all the challenges that come our way, the Scriptures do indicate that *God created this situation* to show his glory and strength to those who were in opposition (Exodus 14:4) and also to the Israelites themselves. And this is indeed what happened—eventually. But in the meantime, the Israelites were stuck and Moses was in a tough spot.

LEARNING TO KEEP STILL

This is the moment where we begin to see more clearly the relationship between Moses' journey into solitude and his effectiveness as a spiritual leader. Because of his encounters with God, Moses is now a fundamentally different person. Rather than the brash, impulsive, take-matters-into-my-own-hands kind of leader that he once tried to be, he is now someone who is able to offer a deeply spiritual response in the face of grave danger. He knows that his soul is not going to be strengthened by getting caught up in the people's fears and complaints. Instead he turns inward, to that place where he has learned to seek God, and from that place he delivers this most counterintuitive message. He says, "Do not be afraid, stand firm, and see the deliverance that the Lord will accomplish for you today; for the Egyptians that you see today you shall never see again. The Lord will fight for you, and *you have only to keep still*" (Exodus 14:13-14, emphasis added).

We ought not underestimate the raw human emotion and survival instincts that are at work in this moment. The people were afraid for their lives, as well they should be. They were backed into a corner at this uncrossable sea, and the Egyptians—who had abused and then murdered their children—were now close enough for the Israelites to see the whites of their eyes. The people were threatening mutiny, and all of their survival instincts were kicking in.

When people get pushed to the edge of their fear like this it can easily become a frightening and out-of-control situation. We've all heard horror stories of human stampedes at sporting events and in crowded public places when people feel that there is a threat of violence or danger. What happens in moments like this is a very primal human response that is exacerbated by a herd mentality. The Israelites were on the brink of this kind of disaster. When a leader starts to feel this kind of dynamic take over, it is an alarming thing and one where great wisdom is required.

Moses' effectiveness in this moment had to do with the fact that even though he was fully aware of the people's emotion, he was even more attuned to the reality of God's presence. He knew that the first thing he needed to do was to help the people *still themselves* and learn to wait on God even in the face of their greatest fear. It reminds me of a scene from the movie *Braveheart* when William Wallace is leading his ragtag band of Scottish soldiers into battle for the first time. It is a situation very similar to Moses' situation. They, too, have come to a turning point where they are willing to do whatever it takes to gain their freedom. They, too, have no weapons, no chariots, no horses, no uniforms, none of the accoutrements of war that the opposing army has. All they have is homemade spears that they needed to throw at just the right time, and they have to wait for Wallace's command. They know that timing was everything. If they throw these crude javelins too soon, they will fall in front of the opposing army; if they wait too long, the spears will sail over their opponents' heads.

The opposing army comes thundering toward them. In the faces of these untrained Scottish soldiers one sees a combination of alertness, fear, readiness, courage and will. Wallace is shouting "Hold! Hold! Hold!" and as a spectator you are wondering if they will have the restraint to wait for exactly the right moment to launch their spears. Will they trust their leader enough to wait when their lives are in danger and everything in them screams to *do something*?

They do hold! They wait until Wallace gives the word, and then they launch their spears. The homemade weapons find their mark, and the opposing army—with all of its wartime accoutrements—turns tail and runs.

TRAINING IN WAITING

What kind of leader is able to call people to wait on God in the face of real threat, when all of their survival instincts are raging? What inner strength does a leader need to be able to access in order to stay calm, to quiet the primal instincts of others, and to create space for turning to God in the midst of such fierce human reactivity? Only a leader who has waited for God in the darkest moments of his own deep need. Only a leader who has stood still and waited for God's deliverance in the places where she feared for her very life. Only the leader with inner spiritual authority that comes from his own waiting can ask others to do the same.

Moses was a man who had been trained in solitude. In this boot camp of the soul, he learned the restraint of waiting for the right time. Even after he heard God's call, he did not jump the gun and return to Egypt too soon. He waited for God's instruction, and it took a very long time. Finally (and this would have taken years), God had said to him, "Go back to Egypt; for all those who were seeking your life are dead" (Exodus 4:19). To wait until all those who oppose you are dead is a pretty good strategy in some cases!

But most of us have not had much training in waiting—or at least not enough to prepare us to help others wait in times when they feel highly threatened. Richard Rohr calls this waiting place "liminal space"; *liminal* comes from the Latin word *limina*, which means threshold. Liminal space, the place of waiting, is

> a unique spiritual position where human beings hate to be but where the biblical God is always leading them. It is when you have left the tried and true, but have not yet been able to replace it with anything else. It is when you are finally out of the way. It is when you are between your old comfort zone and any possible new answer. If you are not trained in how to hold anxiety, how to live with ambiguity, how to entrust and wait, you will run . . . anything to flee this terrible cloud of unknowing.

In solitude we learn to wait on God for our own life so that when our leadership brings us to the place where *the only option* for us as a people is to wait on God, we believe it all the way down to the bottom of our being. Because we have met God in the waiting place (rather than running away or giving in to panic or deceiving ourselves into thinking things are better than they are), we are able to stand firm and believe God in a way that makes it possible for others to follow suit.

It is a sobering thing to ask ourselves this question: *Have I learned enough about how to wait on God in my own life to be able to call others to wait when that is what's truly needed? Have I done enough spiritual journeying to lead people on this part of their journey?*

PRACTICE

As you begin your time in solitude, take a few moments to breathe deeply and become aware of God's presence within you and all around you. As you inhale, breathe in the life that God is giving you in this moment, and as you exhale, release the distractions that keep you from being fully present to God in this moment.

As you feel ready, reflect on your own journey through the lens of the Israelites' exodus from Egypt. What stage most resonates with where you experience yourself right now? If you have a strong sense of where you are on the journey, go back to that section, reread it and listen for what God wants to say to you about your place on the journey.

In your personal spiritual life or in your leadership, have you reached a challenge or an impasse that defies human answers or where those around you are starting to panic? Is it possible that this is a place where God is calling you and those you are leading to be still and allow God to fight for you—or at least to wait for his clear command? In silence, take a few moments to settle into the training of waiting.

■   ■   ■

For the darkness of waiting
of not knowing what is to come
of staying ready and quiet and attentive,
we praise you, O God:

For the darkness and the light
are both alike to you.

For the darkness of staying silent
for the terror of having nothing to say
and for the greater terror
of needing to say nothing,
we praise you, O God.

For the darkness and the light
are both alike to you.

For the darkness of choosing
when you give us the moment
to speak, and act, and change,
and we cannot know what we have set in motion, but we still have
    to take the risk,
we praise you, O God:

For the darkness and the light
are both alike to you.

For the darkness of hoping
in a world which longs for you,
for the wrestling and laboring of all creation
for wholeness and justice and freedom,
we praise you, O God.

For the darkness and the light
are both alike to you.

JANET MORLEY, *BREAD OF TOMORROW*

7

LIVING
WITHIN LIMITS

What you are doing is not good.

You will surely wear yourself out, both you

and these people with you. For the task is too

heavy for you; you cannot do it alone.

EXODUS 18:17-18

Moses was a great leader, but he had to learn, as we all do, how to find a way of life that works. The negative effects of the way that Moses was carrying out his leadership responsibilities seemed to just sneak up on him—as they do for most of us. The first hint that Moses' life in leadership had become unworkable was that early in the journey he sent his young family back home to Midian to live with his father-in-law, Jethro. Not a good sign: evidently his lifestyle was not sane enough to include a wife and children.

Jethro was the first person to challenge Moses' lifestyle. When the Israelites' journey brought them into closer proximity, he brought Zipporah and the boys back to Moses. During this visit Jethro, who was an experienced spiritual leader himself, affirmed the evidence of God's blessing on Moses' leadership, but he also observed one of Moses' blind spots. Every day Moses sat as a judge for all the people, and they stood around waiting for him to judge their cases from morning until night. It was very a chaotic and exhausting process for everyone involved, and when Jethro witnessed this debacle he confronted it immediately. "What are you *doing?*" he asked. "Why do you sit alone, while all the people stand around you from morning until evening?" (see Exodus 18:14).

Moses' answer betrayed a touch of that oh-so-satisfying feeling of indispensability: "Because the people come to *me* to inquire of God. When they have a dispute, they come to *me* . . . and *I* make known to them the statutes and instructions of God" (18:15-16, emphasis added). Oh how subtle are the inner dynamics that allow us to become caught in a pace of life that is unlivable! And oh how desperately we need a Jethro in our lives to point out that there is another way.

Jethro did not mince words or even attempt to be diplomatic. He came right out and told Moses that what he was doing was not good—for himself or for the people who were seeking spiritual assistance—and that he was on a sure path to spiritual exhaustion. Yes, it *was* Moses' job to represent the people before God, but to handle all the cases himself was a load that was too heavy for one person to bear. Jethro told Moses that he needed to surround himself with other spiritual leaders who could handle the bulk of the cases, setting up a process whereby only the most important and complicated cases would be referred to him.

WHAT YOU ARE DOING IS NOT GOOD

It is a very humbling moment in the life of a leader when we realize that we have taken on too much. It requires us to call into question the cultural stereotypes that venerate the rugged individualist who can do it all by himself. It challenges us to confront the grandiosity that got us where we are in the first place. And even when we do get around to admitting the problem, it might take even longer to do something decisive about it! We hold out as long as we can, unwilling to admit that we cannot do it alone, that there is something about our life that is just not working. At some point we are brought face to face with our human limitations. We

> *When you reach the limits of your resources or abilities,*
>
> *you have no margin left. Yet because we*
>
> *don't even know what margin is, we don't realize it is gone.*
>
> *We know that something is not right*
>
> *but we can't solve the puzzle beyond that. Our pain*
>
> *is palpable, but our assailant remains unnamed.*
>
> RICHARD SWENSON, *MARGIN*

realize that we are not the Energizer bunny. We cannot keep going and going and going. There is a limit.

Sometimes a leader has been going so fast for so long that they don't know how close to their limits they are. Or they are so convinced that this is what life in leadership requires that they think they don't have any other option. But we don't always have a Jethro to point out the problem before it is too late. In the absence of a Jethro in our life, it can be very helpful for us to learn to recognize signs—in ourselves and others—that we may be reaching our limit so that we can pull back and recalibrate as Moses did. Following are a few of the symptoms that might manifest themselves when we are dangerously depleted and may be functioning beyond human limitations.

- *Irritability or hypersensitivity.* Things that normally wouldn't bother us (such as a child's mistake, another driver cutting us off in traffic or a coworker's irritating habit) put us over the edge. We may or may not express our rage outwardly, but inwardly we are aware of reactions that are all out of proportion to the event itself.

- *Restlessness.* During waking hours we might be aware of a vague sense that something is not quite right or an even stronger feeling of wanting to bolt from our life. When it is time to rest, we might find ourselves unable to settle down and sit quietly or fall asleep. Because we are overstimulated, our sleep may be broken, marred by too much mental activity or disturbing dreams.

- *Compulsive overworking.* "Overwork is this decade's cocaine, the problem without a name," says Bryan Robinson, who has written widely about the phenomenon and estimates that as many as 25 percent of Americans have this addiction. "Workaholism is an obsessive-compulsive disorder," he writes, "that manifests itself through self-imposed demands, an inability to regulate work habits, and an overindulgence in work—to the exclusion of most other life activities." This compulsive behavior can also manifest itself in a frenetic quality to our work. We might find that we are unable to stop or slow down even when that would be appropriate—like at night after dinner or on vacation. A compulsive leader is one who—for some reason that he or she cannot quite name—has no boundaries on work, checks e-mail late into the evening, and is unable to unplug completely to go on vacation, to enter into solitude or to spend uninterrupted time with family.

- *Emotional numbness.* When we are pushing our limit, we may notice that we can't feel anything—good or bad. It takes energy to experience and process a full range of human emotion. When we are "at capacity" we literally do not have the energy to engage the full range of human experience, including our emotions. In addition, we might be afraid that if we did stop and experience our emotions we would be overwhelmed, and who has time for that?

- *Escapist behaviors.* When we do have a break in the action, we might notice that increasingly we are succumbing to escapist behaviors (such as compulsive eating, drinking or other substance abuse, spending, television, pornography, surfing the Internet) and don't have the energy to choose activities that are life giving (such as exercising, going for a walk or bike ride, connecting meaningfully with friends and family, enjoying a hobby or interest like playing an instrument, cooking, painting, drawing, writing poetry, playing sports, working with our hands, reading a good book). This becomes a vicious cycle, because escapist behaviors actually drain energy from us—energy that we could use to make life-giving choices—and then we just get more and more lethargic.

- *Disconnected from our identity and calling.* More and more we find ourselves going through the motions of doing ministry but disconnected from a true sense of who we are and what God is calling us to do. Increasingly, we find that we are at the mercy of other people's expectations and our own inner compulsions because we lack an internal plumb line against which to measure these demands.

- *Not able to attend to human needs.* We don't have time to take care of basic human needs such as exercise, eating right, sleeping enough, going to the doctor, having that minor (or major) surgery we need.

Even such simple things as getting the car washed, picking up the dry cleaning or staying organized seem impossible to accomplish, indicating that we're pushing the limits of being human. We may also notice that our most important relationships (family and friends) are routinely being short-changed.

- *Hoarding energy.* When we are running on empty, we can have the inner experience of always feeling threatened, as though exposing ourselves to additional people or situations would drain the last of our energy or the energy we are trying to conserve for what we think is important. We might actually become overly self-protective and even reclusive in our attempts to hoard the few resources we do have. In their book *The Power of Full Engagement,* Jim Loehr and Tony Schwartz call this *defense spending.*

- *Slippage in our spiritual practices.* Practices that are normally life-giving (solitude and silence, prayer, personal reflection on Scripture, journaling, self-examination, caring for the body) become burdensome, and we don't have energy for them even though we know they are good for us. We might even find that we are so accustomed to using God and Scripture for ministry purposes that we no longer know how to be with God for ourselves personally. We know that there are things we need to attend to in God's presence, but we truly do not have the energy or the will. Over time, this becomes a symptom and also a source of our depletion.

If even a few of these symptoms are true for you, chances are you are pushing up against human limitations and you, too, might need to consider that "what you are doing is not good" for you or for the people you are serving.

SHARING THE LOAD

When Moses reached this point in his own life, it took a reorganization of the whole leadership structure to address the fact that Moses was carrying too much of the burden alone. Part of the answer was for him to delegate responsibilities to other capable individuals and then to trust that they could carry them out.

The individuals who would bear this burden with Moses could not be just anyone. They needed to be people who feared God—people who were spiritual and had a vibrant relationship with God—not just people who demonstrated competence in a particular area. They needed to be trustworthy in every way, living their lives honestly before God and others. There was no ambiguity in Jethro's counsel: sharing the load with other spiritual people was *the only way* Moses would be able to remain faithful to his calling to leadership over the long haul. This change was not for Moses' benefit alone; the people would also benefit, because they would be able to find resolution of their conflicts in a timely fashion.

Learning how to handle his responsibilities in ways that were sane and doable for himself, his family, and the people around him was an ongoing process that required attention throughout Moses' life. To his credit, he was very teachable about it all. He listened and followed Jethro's advice, appointing judges to help handle the people's disputes, and his load was lightened—at least for a time. In so doing, he learned a lesson that we all must learn: that to be human is to have limits.

All true leaders must eventually face this reality, or they will break themselves against an immovable wall. There are physical limits of time and space, strength and energy. There are limits to our relational capacities, depending on our personality type. There are the limits associated with this particular season of my life. There are the limits of this particular community and this particular set of relationships. There are the limits of *this* calling that God has placed on my life, which means that I am not available for other callings.

BEYOND GRANDIOSITY

I have spent much of my life bumping up against limits, ignoring limits and pretending there are no limits. It is an embarrassing little secret that seems to be common among leaders, and we probably need to be more honest about it. Buried deep in the psyche of many leaders is a Superman mentality—that somehow there are a few of us who can function beyond normal human limitations and save the world. Or at least our little corner of the world. This is a grandiosity that we indulge to our own peril.

Paul, the quintessential activist leader, actually wrote about living within limits in a passage that I somehow avoided all my life until I stumbled upon it quite by accident. It was at the beginning of a planning day with the executive team of the Transforming Center, and we began our day—as we always did—with morning prayer, which includes following the lectionary schedule for reading Scripture. As usual, there was more on the agenda than we could realistically expect to get done in one day, and we were facing some significant directional decisions. I, for one, was ready to get on with it and could easily have been tempted to forgo morning prayers so we could get right to it. Fortunately, the power of our prayer disciplines prevailed.

The New Testament reading for the day was 2 Corinthians 10:12-17 in which Paul talks about the danger of comparing ourselves to others and measuring ourselves against their accomplishments. His antidote for this all-too-human tendency was to learn to stay within the limits of his own life and calling. He says, "We, however, will not boast beyond limits, but will keep within the field that God has assigned to us, to reach out even as far as you. For we were not overstepping our limits when we reached you. . . . We do not boast beyond limits, that is, in the labors of others; but our hope is that, as your faith increases, our sphere of action among you may be greatly enlarged" (2 Corinthians 10:13-15).

Until that very moment I had never realized that Paul used the word *limits* three times in just a few verses and that he seemed to be very clear about the limits and boundaries of his calling. He knew the field God had given him to work, and he knew better than to go outside it.

He knew that there was a sphere of action and influence that had been given to him by God, and he would not go beyond it *unless God enlarged his field.*

Paul seemed to grapple honestly with the reality of limitations in several different ways in his writings, and, in fact, this seemed to be part of his maturing as a leader who was both gifted and called. When he wrote about not thinking more highly of ourselves than we ought (Romans 12:3), he was making a very general statement about limiting our grandiosity and pride by cultivating a realistic sense of our essential nature. He was talking about being willing to live *within the limits and the possibilities of who we really are.* As he matured, he revealed a very personal understanding that his deep struggle with a thorn in the flesh was a gift that was given to him to limit *his own* grandiosity and keep him in touch with his humanness. In 2 Corinthians 4 he talked about what it is like to carry the treasure of ministry in fragile, earthen vessels. He wrote poignantly from his experience of his own human limitations and his conviction that it is precisely in our willingness to carry God's luminous presence in such fragile containers—without pretending to be anything more than what we are—that the power of God can be most clearly seen.

On this particular day there could not have been a better Scripture for our fledgling organization and its intrepid leaders! In the silence that followed the reading, it occurred to me that maybe I had never really faced the possibility that there might be real limits to my life and person and that my refusal to live within limits was one of the reasons I was in such an exhausted state. This is not the kind of thing visionary leaders talk about, and yet here was Paul spelling it out in the clearest of terms.

In that silence I also had to admit that I did not have this same clarity or the same willingness to live within limits that Paul had. In my own heart were visions of grandeur that might or might not have had anything to do with the sphere of action that God had actually marked out for us as an organization. Within my own heart was the tendency to look longingly at someone else's field and wish that mine were a little more like theirs. In a rush of self-awareness, I realized that the ramped-up feelings I brought into our planning days had sometimes had to do with my own ego-driven plans rather than an ability to be at peace within the field that God had placed me in.

This passage changed my prayer going into this particular planning day and in my ministry life overall. My prayer for all of us who gathered to work and plan for the future of our ministry was, "God, help us live within the limits of what you have called us to do. Help us live within the limits of who we *are*—both as individuals and as an organization. Help us give our very best in the field that we have been given to work and to trust you to enlarge our sphere of action if and when you know we are ready. Help us know the difference between being driven by grandiose visions and responding faithfully to the expansion of your work in and through us."

This was a way of praying that I would have resisted had it not come from God himself, but it has become a very healthy way for me to curb my idealism and grandiosity when that is needed. It is another way of living within the parameters of what is real, and it enables me and those who are leading with me to make decisions that honor the limits of our humanness, our life situations and our ministry setting.

THE GRACE OF LIVING WITHIN LIMITS

There is a lot of narcissism among leaders—even Christian ones—and the truth is that we are driven by our grandiosity more than we think. This is not without cause. Christopher Lasch, in his book *The Culture of Narcissism,* makes the sobering observation that narcissism as a personality structure goes hand in hand with bureaucracy, the type of social institution that predominates today. "The narcissist has many traits that make for success in bureaucratic institutions, which put a premium on the manipulation of interpersonal relations, discourage the formation of deep personal attachments, and at the same time provide the narcissist with the approval he needs in order to validate his self-esteem. Although he may resort to therapies that promise to give meaning to life and to overcome his sense of emptiness, in his professional career the narcissist often enjoys considerable success." And as Donald Capps so aptly points out, "Since our churches have taken on many of the characteristics of bureaucracies, it is not surprising that clergy are sometimes rewarded, not punished for their narcissistic behaviors."

One of the ways to recognize narcissism within ourselves is to notice when we have not yet accepted the field, the sphere of action, that God has given us—the opportunities and the limits of life in *this* body, *this* community, *this* set of relationships, *this* financial situation, *this* place where we have been called by God to serve. Narcissistic leaders are always looking longingly at someone else's field as somehow being more worthy or more indicative of success. They are always pushing the limits of their situation rather than lovingly working the field they have been given.

When we refuse to live within limits, we are refusing to live with a basic reality of human existence. There is a finiteness to what I can do in this body. There is a finiteness to how many relationships I can engage in meaningfully at one time. There is a finiteness to time—how many hours there are in a day, how many days there are in a week and how much can be done in those blocks of time. There is a finiteness to my energy. There comes a time when I am tired. There comes a time when I am sick. There comes a time when I am injured. These are times when I am reminded that I am human—a finite being living in the presence of an infinite God. God is the infinite one. God is the one who can be all things to all people. God is the one who can be in all places at once. God is the one who never sleeps. I am not.

Our unwillingness to live within limits—both personally and in community—is one of the deepest sources of depletion and eventual burnout. That's the bad news.

The good news is that there is something deeply spiritual about living and working within our God-ordained limits—or to put it another way, living fully and acceptingly within our own set of realities. The late Christopher Reeve is a stunning example of this. Before a tragic horseback-riding accident in 1995, Reeve seemed to live with few limits. Good-looking, intelligent, athletic, he was the ultimate metaphor for American grandiosity. The Superman character that he brought to life became a contemporary icon for our idealized expectations of what an American hero should be—someone who showed up and saved the world over and over again. The only problem was that none of it was real.

Fast-forward to his life as a quadriplegic and we see a man who is living with the severest of human limitations. Strapped to a wheelchair, reliant on a respirator to breathe, completely dependent on his wife and others for basic care and functioning, now he is a man making a real contribution to the human race. Now all of a sudden life is really real. With the passion that came from having faced one's limitations, he raised funds for medical research, lobbied for insurance reform and participated in cutting-edge rehabilitative exercise therapies. He reached out in friendship and collegiality to many whom he might never have even noticed had it not been for his new limitations. His tenacity benefited many others besides himself—benefits that extended beyond his death.

Of his experience of living with extreme limitation, he commented, "I obviously didn't wish this, but it's amazing. If it hadn't happened, I probably would have been that person that people would say: 'Oh, he's that actor who used to do that thing with the cape.' " Instead he became a person of substance, whom friends and colleagues experienced as a person of courage, intelligence, dignity and generosity.

Living graciously within the boundaries of our life as it has been entrusted to us gives our life substance. Oddly enough, something of the will of God is contained in the very limits that we often try to sidestep or ignore. Living within limits is not in any way an acquiescence that is despairing, passive or fatalistic. Rather it honors the deepest realities of the life God has given us. Life in this body at this age and stage. Life in my family at its age and stage. Life in this personality. Life with this community. Life in the midst of this calling.

Living within limits is another facet of settling into ourselves that is crucial for soulful, solid leadership. It is another facet of Moses' instruction to the children of Israel in Deuteronomy 30:14, "The word [of God] is very near to you; it is in your mouth and in your heart for you to observe." It is not up in the heavens or across the ocean. It is right here—in this body, in this soul, in this set of circumstances. This is where you will discover the will of God.

PRACTICE

Someone has said that we are not human beings trying to become spiritual but spiritual beings trying to become human. Think about that for a moment. It's true, isn't it? And it raises a great question: How are you doing at being human?

With that question in mind, take a few moments to breathe deeply and pay particular attention to how the awareness of your breathing helps you be attuned to your life in the body. Allow yourself to be at ease for a few moments and experience the soft body of yourself—its limits, its needs, its tender places, its weariness, its vulnerability, its strength. Experience your finiteness and what it feels like to be a finite being in the presence of the infinite God.

Then begin to notice where your leadership experience might be similar to Moses' and where you, too, need to live within limits. Has your way of life become unmanageable to the extent that you have "sent your family away" in some fashion or have not been able to give your best to them or fully include them in your heart and life? Has anyone offered comments on your way of life (as Jethro did) that you need to pay attention to? Are you doing too much of your ministry alone? Is there any way in which your body is trying to speak to you through illness, aches and pains, exhaustion?

Sit with the question that seems most pertinent to you now. Allow the following prayer to guide you into a moment of being with God just as you are, amid the challenges of your leadership setting. Listen for what your heart needs to say to God and what God wants to say to you.

■　■　■

O Eternal One,
it would be easier for me to pray
　if I were clear
　　and of a single mind and pure heart,
　if I could be done hiding from myself
　　and from you, even in my prayers.
But I am who I am,
　mixture of motives and excuses,
　　blur of memories
　　　quiver of hopes,
　knot of fear,
　　tangle of confusion,
　　　and restless with love
　　　　for love . . .
Come, find me, Lord.
Be with me exactly as I am.
Help me find me, Lord.
　Help me accept what I am
　　so I can begin to be yours.

TED LODER, *GUERRILLAS OF GRACE*

8

SPIRITUAL RHYTHMS IN THE LIFE OF THE LEADER

Morning by morning they gathered [manna],

as much as each needed. . . .

"See! The LORD has given you the sabbath."

EXODUS 16:21, 29

Several years ago, during a time when I was not officially on staff at any church, we had the opportunity to simply attend a local church as a family. With three teenagers/young adults, it was a busy season of our lives, yet we really wanted to establish rhythms that gave us one day a week for rest, renewal and being together in a relaxed and uninterrupted way. Given work, school and sports schedules, Sunday was the only possible day that we might have been able to set aside as qualitatively different from other days of the week. But in addition to typical obstacles to creating such a day created by secular culture, we made the sad discovery that the church itself was a major obstacle to creating a sabbath rhythm. Committee meetings, youth group events, choir practices, elder meetings, small group gatherings and congregational meetings were all scheduled on Sundays, which meant that most Sundays found our family coming and going all day, unable to even schedule a meal together.

It is hard for me to put into words how discouraging this was, how defeating. I knew that sabbath keeping was particularly challenging for pastors and other church staff, but now I was shocked to discover that even for normal participants the church itself was making it difficult to keep a sabbath—a discipline that I have come to believe is foundational to a life well lived in God's presence. How I longed for a community of faith that would help us—by our very participation in it—to live into the rhythms that our hearts were longing for.

Contrast our contemporary reality with the leadership that God asks Moses to provide for the Hebrew community in Exodus 16. Part of Moses' job as a spiritual leader was to establish rhythms for life in community that would sustain the people and help them live as human beings in the presence of Almighty God. First of all there were daily rhythms of receiving their sustenance from the hand of God—quail in the evening and manna in the morning. "Morning by morning they gathered it," as much as they needed for that day.

Beyond these daily rhythms, their very identity as a nation was to be shaped by rhythms that involved working for six days and then resting on the sabbath. Before the Ten Commandments were even given, instructions about the sabbath were made very clear, and Moses' job was to lead the way in its observance. In preparation for that very first sabbath, Moses gave careful instructions to the leaders so that they could help guide the people in understanding what was happening. "Tomorrow is a day of solemn rest, a holy sabbath to the LORD" (Exodus 16:23). And it didn't come easily. The people just didn't get it at first. But Moses was right there to help them along. Even after they got confused and made mistakes, Moses kept reiterating the significance of this important way of life. " 'See! The LORD has given you the sabbath, therefore on the sixth day he gives you food for two days; each of you stay where you are; do not leave your place on the seventh day.' So the people rested on the seventh day" (vv. 29-30).

Little by little under Moses' shepherding care, the people learned how to enter into this shared discipline that built lessons about trust into the very rhythm of their lives. Every week the whole community entered into this exercise in trust together. Every week the community gave in to their need for rest, believing that if they did this God would continue to care for their needs. Every week the whole community used the space created by not working to turn itself toward God. Through this very concrete discipline, they lived out their belief that somehow the work they could accomplish in six days would be enough and God could be trusted with running the world while they rested. This daily and weekly rhythm was their earliest pattern for their life together in God's presence, and it shaped their identity as individual souls and as a community. It taught them how to honor God with the time of their lives.

THE BONDAGE OF BUSYNESS

For the Israelites, incorporating these rhythms involved a radical reordering of life as they had known it. Clearly we contemporary Chris-

> *We are blessed with inner rhythms that tell us where we are,*
>
> *and where we are going. No matter, then,*
>
> *our fifty and sixty hour work weeks, the refusing*
>
> *to stop for lunch, the bypassing sleep and working deep*
>
> *into the darkness. If we stop, if we return to rest,*
>
> *our natural state reasserts itself.*
>
> *Our natural wisdom and balance come to our aid,*
>
> *and we can find our way to what is good, necessary and true.*
>
> WAYNE MULLER, *SABBATH*

tians do not have a handle on this. A recent survey of twenty thousand Christians around the world revealed that many identify busyness and constant overload as a major distraction from God. Michael Zigarelli, who conducted this survey from his post as associate professor of management at the Charleston University School of Business, describes "a vicious cycle" prompted by cultural conformity. He says, "It may be the case that 1) Christians are assimilating a culture of busyness, hurry and overload, which leads to 2) God becoming more marginalized in Christians' lives, which leads to 3) a deteriorating relationship with God, which leads to 4) Christians becoming even more vulnerable to adopting secular assumptions about how to live, which leads to 5) more conformity to a culture of busyness, hurry and overload. And then the cycle begins again."

This in itself is a sad state of affairs, but it gets worse. Tellingly, this survey reveals that pastors and Christian leaders seem to be as caught up in the culture of busyness as anyone else. A full 65 percent of pastors (right up there with lawyers, managers and nurses) are among the most likely to rush from task to task in a way that interferes with their relationship with God. "It's tragic. It's ironic," notes Zigarelli, "that the very people who could best help us escape the bondage of busyness are themselves in chains."

The sad truth is that life in and around the church these days often leads people into a way of life that is becoming more and more layered with Christian busyness. If we are honest, we might admit that Christian leaders are just as driven to succeed as anyone else, only our success is measured in larger congregations, better church services, more innovations and bigger buildings. There is nothing wrong with any of these things in and of themselves, but what *can be* wrong is the kind of life we have to live in order to make them happen. The operative word here is *driven*.

Everywhere I travel these days, those who are involved in church work and parachurch ministry report that they are exhausted in ministry and have despaired of finding a way of life that works. Many, in their more honest moments, dream of leaving ministry altogether, having come to the conclusion that this is the only way out of an unworkable lifestyle. As one pastor reported, "I am always sixty seconds away from running for the mountains." We are becoming increasingly aware of the fact that no matter how much one spiritualizes it, Christian busyness must not be confused with the Christian spiritual life or with a Christian's experience of God.

Jesus himself seemed to understand how quickly our passions, even the most noble ones, can wear us out if we're not careful. Early in his ministry with the disciples, he began to teach them about the importance of establishing sane rhythms of work and rest. In Mark 6, Jesus had just commissioned the disciples for ministry and had given them the authority to cast out demons, preach the gospel and heal the sick. After completing their first ministry excursion, they returned excited about their newfound powers and crowded around Jesus to report on all they had done and taught.

But Jesus didn't have much time for their ministry reports. Immediately he instructed them, "Come away to a deserted place all by yourselves and rest a while" (Mark 6:31). He seemed to be more concerned with helping them to establish rhythms that would sustain them in ministry than he was in their ministry reports. He was more interested in helping them not to become overly enamored by ministry successes or inordinately driven by their compulsions to do more than he was in sending them back out to do ministry.

When we keep pushing forward without taking adequate time for rest and replenishment, our way of life may seem heroic, but there is a frenetic quality to our work that lacks true effectiveness because we have lost the ability to be present to God, to be present to other people and to discern what is really needed in our situation. The result can be "sloppy desperation": a mental and spiritual lethargy that prevents the quality of presence that would deliver true insight and spiritual leadership.

Charles, a gifted physician, illustrates the point:

> I discovered in medical school that if I saw a patient when I was tired or overworked, I would order a lot of tests. I was so exhausted, I couldn't tell exactly what was going on . . . so I got in the habit of ordering a battery of tests, hoping they would tell me what I was missing. But when I was rested—if I had the opportunity to get some sleep, or go for a quiet walk—when I saw the next patient, I could rely on my intuition and experience to give me a pretty accurate reading of what was happening. . . . When I could take the time to listen and be present with them and their illness, I was almost always right.

When we are depleted, we become overly reliant on voices outside of ourselves to tell us what is going on. We react to symptoms rather than seeking to understand and respond to underlying causes. We rely on other people's ministry models and outside consultants because we are too tired to listen in our setting and craft something that is uniquely

> *Sadly, the need for recovery is often viewed*
>
> *as evidence of weakness rather than an integral aspect*
>
> *of sustained performance. The result is*
>
> *that we give almost no attention to renewing and expanding*
>
> *our energy reserves, individually or organizationally.*
>
> *To maintain a powerful pulse in our lives, we must learn*
>
> *how to rhythmically spend and renew energy.*
>
> JIM LOEHR AND TONY SCHWARTZ, *THE POWER OF FULL ENGAGEMENT*

suited to meet the needs that are there. When we are rested, however, we bring steady, alert attention that is characterized by true discernment about what is truly needed in our situation, and the energy and creativity to carry it out.

RHYTHMS OF WORK AND REST

Rhythms of work and rest are fundamental to our well-being. In their book *The Power of Full Engagement*, Jim Loehr and Tony Schwartz note that alternating periods of activity with periods of rest has been a means of maximizing performance among athletes since Flavius Philostratus wrote training manuals for Greek athletes in A.D. 170-245. Balancing stress and recovery is the key to managing energy not only for competitive athletes but also for all of us.

Following a period of activity, the body must replenish fundamental biochemical sources of energy. This is called "compensation" and when it occurs, energy expended is recovered. Increase the intensity of the training or performance demand, and it is necessary to increase the amount of energy renewal. . . . The same is true organizationally. To the degree that leaders and managers build cultures around continuous work—whether that means several-hour meetings, or long days, or the expectation that people work in the evenings and on weekends—performance is necessarily compromised over time. Cultures that encourage people to seek intermittent renewal not only inspire greater commitment, but also greater productivity.

While it may be a little uncomfortable to use the language of performance in reference to spiritual leadership, let us not allow language to distract us. As pastors and ministry leaders, we want to give our best to our calling. We want to run the race we have been given to run to the best of our ability. We want to last for the long haul. There is nothing more crucial to the staying power of the leader than establishing rhythms that keep us replenished—body, mind and soul. There is nothing more crucial than rhythms that help us make ourselves available to God for the work that only he can do in us—day in and day out. Week in and week out. Year in and year out. All organisms follow life-sustaining rhythms. If we believe that we are somehow above or beyond or immune to our need for such rhythms, we will find ourselves in danger.

Sabbath keeping is the linchpin of a life lived in sync with the rhythms that God himself built into our world, and yet it is the discipline that seems hardest for us to live. Sabbath keeping honors the body's need for rest, the spirit's need for replenishment and the soul's need to delight itself in God for God's own sake. It begins with willingness to acknowledge the limits of our humanness and then to take steps to live more graciously within the order of things.

And the first order of things is that we are creatures and God is the Creator. God is the one who is infinite; I, on the other hand, must learn to live within the physical limits of time and space and the human limits of my own strength and energy. There are limits to my relational, emotional, mental and spiritual capacities. I am not God. God is the only one who can be all things to all people. God is the only one who can be two places at once. God is the one who never sleeps. I am not. We can't remind ourselves of this enough. This is pretty basic stuff, but many of us live as though we don't know it.

Sabbath keeping may be the most challenging rhythm for leaders to establish because Sunday in most churches has become a day of Christian busyness—and of course, the busiest person on that day is the pastor! This means that pastors need to set aside another day for their sabbath. Or they might consider ordering their church's life so that everyone learns how to practice sabbath. It could begin with worship, but then everyone goes home and rests and delights for the rest of the day because there are no other church activities. In that way, the leader's commitment to sabbath becomes a blessing for everyone. (For a more complete discussion of sabbath keeping, see chapter eight of my book *Sacred Rhythms* [Downers Grove, Ill.: InterVarsity Press, 2006].)

RHYTHMS OF ENGAGEMENT AND RETREAT

One of the most important rhythms for a person in ministry is to establish a constant back-and-forth motion between engagement and retreat—times when we are engaged in the battle, giving our best energy to taking the next hill, and times when we step back in order to gain perspective, restrategize and tend our wounds—an inevitability of life in ministry. If an army keeps slogging it out on the battlefield without taking time to regroup, it is doomed to defeat. And so it is with the Christian leader-warrior.

One of the occupational hazards for those of us in Christian ministry is that it can become hard to distinguish between the times when we are "on" and working *for* God and times when we can just *be with* God for our own soul's sake. We might notice that Scripture has been reduced to a textbook or a tool for ministry rather than an intimate personal communication from God to us. Perhaps prayer has become an exhausting round of different kinds of mental activity or a public display of our spiritual prowess.

Times of extended retreat give us a chance to come home to ourselves in God's presence and to bring the realities of our life to God in utter privacy. This is important for us and for those we serve. When we repress what is real in our life and just keep soldiering on, we get weary from holding it in, and eventually it leaks out in ways that are damaging to ourselves and to others. But on retreat there is time and space to attend to what is real in my own life—to celebrate the joys, grieve the losses, shed tears, sit with the questions, feel my anger, attend to my loneliness—and allow God to be with me in those places. These are not times for problem-solving or fixing, because not everything can be fixed or solved. On retreat we rest in God and wait on him to do what is needed. Eventually we return to the battle with fresh energy and keener insight.

SILENCE AND WORD, STILLNESS AND ACTION

"When there are many words, transgression is unavoidable," the Scriptures say (Proverbs 10:19 NASB). This is a truth that could drive leaders to despair, given the incessant flow of words from our mouths, pens and computers. Those of us who deal in words are at great risk of misusing words and even sinning with our words due to the sheer volume of them. I don't know about you, but sometimes I can literally feel—deep in my bones—that if I do not shut my mouth for a while I will get myself in trouble, because my words will be completely disconnected from the reality of God in my life.

Silence is the only cure for this desperate situation. "Right speech comes out of silence, and right silence comes out of speech," says Dietrich Bonhoeffer. In silence our speech patterns are refined, because silence fosters a self-awareness that enables us to choose more aptly the words that we say. Rather than speech that issues from subconscious needs to impress, to put others in their place, to compete, control and manipulate, to put a good spin on things, we are able to notice our inner dynamics and make choices that are grounded in love, trust and God-given wisdom.

The psalmist says, "When you are disturbed, do not sin; ponder it on your beds, and be silent. Offer right sacrifices [in other words, stay faithful to your spiritual practices], and put your trust in the LORD" (Psalm 4:4-5). There are times when the most heroic thing a leader can do is to remain in that private place with God for as long as it takes to keep from sinning. In silence we consciously trust ourselves to God rather than following our human impulses to fix, control or put people in their place.

Engaging in rhythms of silence and stillness that eventually give way to well-chosen words and right action is a pattern that teaches us in very concrete ways to wait on God. This doesn't come easily for those of us who are busy trying to make things happen. It takes energy to be restrained and to wait for the work of God in our life and in the world around us. *The more we are called upon to use words, the more distressing things are, the more that active leadership is required of us, the more silence we need.* The greater the call for decisive action, the more we must be sure that we have waited long enough to receive clear direction.

This was a rhythm that Moses had learned so well that when the challenges of leadership came, his first response was to be still and wait (as he instructed the people at the Red Sea) until he recognized God's instruction. His action emerged from a clear sense of what he had heard from God. When God's instruction came for the Israelites to move forward and for Moses to lift his staff and stretch out his hand so that the water would divide, it was the exactly right thing to do. But it was something they would have never thought up on their own. Moses would not have known to do this had he not been orienting himself internally to God and waiting until God's guidance was clear.

The key to the efficacy of rhythms is to understand that either one without the other would be less than adequate. If we pray and never do anything, God's will will never actually be done. If we keep doing things but shun stillness and prayer, chances are our actions will be less than what is really needed. It is the rhythm of silence and action that makes it good.

SELF-KNOWLEDGE AND SELF-EXAMINATION

A natural outcome of time spent in the safety of God's presence is that it becomes quite natural to engage routinely in a rhythm of celebrating who we are in Christ and the work of transformation that God is doing in our lives, as well as inviting him to show us those places where we are still living in bondage to sin and negative patterns. Without the regular experience of being received and loved by God in solitude and silence, we are vulnerable to a kind of leadership that is driven by profound emptiness that we are seeking to fill through performance and achievement. This unconscious striving is very dangerous for us and for those around us; it will eventually burn us out (since there is no amount of achievement that will ultimately satisfy the emptiness of the human soul), and the people we work with will eventually notice that they are mere cogs in the wheel of our own ego-driven plans.

It takes profound willingness to invite God to search us and know us at the deepest level of our being, allowing him to show us the difference between the performance-oriented drivenness of the false self and the deeper calling to lead from our authentic self in God. There is an elemental chaos that gets stirred up when we have been in God's presence enough that we can recognize pretense and performance and every other thing that bolsters our sense of self. It is unnerving to see evidence that these patterns are still at work—perhaps just a bit more subtly—in our everyday lives.

When we are stripped of external distraction in solitude, we inevitably become more aware of false patterns of thinking and being and doing that usually lurk unnoticed under the surface busyness of our lives. Inevitably, we will become more aware of how these patterns have shaped our leadership. Perhaps we glimpse an ego-driven self that is bent on control and image management. Perhaps we see an empty self that is hungry to fill itself with the approval and accolades of others. Perhaps we see a broken self desperately seeking to preserve the illusion that we have it all together. Or maybe we see a wounded self that has spent untold energy seeking healing where healing cannot be found.

It is impossible to overstate how dangerous we can become as leaders if we are not routinely inviting God to search us and know us and lead us in a new way. It is impossible to overstate how needy we ourselves can become if we do not have times for allowing the healing love of God to touch our brokenness in ways that can restore us to health and wholeness. The journey of self-knowledge that leads us beyond the false self to living and leading from our authentic self is a challenging one, but it is eminently worth it. This is the kind of truth that ultimately sets us free to lead from a truer self, one that is compelled by truer motivations that God placed within us before the foundations of the earth.

FINDING A WAY OF LIFE TOGETHER

Moses' leadership was not only about leading the people to the Promised Land; it was also about guiding them into a way of life that was good for them in the here and now. Lessons about how to live well were to be discovered in community with others who were seeking the same goodness. Such learning could only be guided by one who was discovering this goodness for himself. This is an important aspect of leadership that is often lost on those who see visions and dream dreams.

When we are seeking a way of life that is counter to the dominant culture (as the Israelites were then and as we are today), we need support. We need a community to practice with, a community that by our participation in it shapes our lives in positive ways. This understanding is deeply embedded in Christian tradition, as. St. Benedict and other saints developed what they called "a rule of life" to help monks who were living together in monasteries seek God and live responsibly in the world.

St. Benedict's Rule, like any rule of life, is simply a pattern of attitudes, behaviors and practices that are regular and routine and are intended to produce a certain quality of life and character in us. Even though St. Benedict's Rule was written around fifteen hundred years ago, there has been an amazing resurgence of interest in it; much has been written recently about its relevance to contemporary culture. This reflects a deep longing for a way of life that works which seems to be sweeping our culture—the very longing and need that God met for the Israelites in guiding Moses to establish rhythms for them.

Once we get caught up in leadership roles of responsibilities and accountabilities, it is easy to lose sight of an all-important question: what are we really inviting people into when we invite them to join us on the spiritual journey? With all of our emphasis on external signs of progress, it is easy to lose sight of the fact that we are not primarily inviting people into our plans and schemes. We are inviting them into a life-giving way of life in God.

When individuals enter into the deeper dynamics of the spiritual journey and begin attending to what is really required for them to be well, but the community of which they are a part is not grappling with these issues together, a terrible dissonance can develop. The pace of life in the community may set them up to make decisions that they don't want to make and ask questions they don't want to ask. *Do I remain a part of this community where the way of life is killing me, or do I leave in order to survive as a human being? What defense structures do I need to put in place to defend against the influence of this community rather than being able to lean into it and learn from it?*

Human beings in community are like rocks in a riverbed; we are shaped by the flow of life in the communities we are a part of. Part of our calling as leaders is to be brave enough to ask the question, *How does life in this community shape me and shape others—in this case, around issues related to living within human limits?* For a community to begin living within limits, there must be a willingness to name current reality, to envision a healthier reality and then to make plans that will take the community from one to the other. This takes real spiritual leadership, given the many cultural, psychological and even spiritual dynamics (spiritual warfare) that work against it.

Rhythms designed to foster a way of life in community that is deeply good for the human soul as it embarks on the deeper spiritual journey are not established by accident. The process is led in very practical ways by leaders who are living within limits themselves, who are in touch with their own humanity and wrestling honestly with the realities of their own life. There is no way to circumvent the personal honesty and struggle that are required in order to lead others in this way with integrity. It is not good enough to say, "Don't do as I do, do as I say." In this case, our lives must speak before our mouths do.

COURAGEOUS LEADERSHIP

The process of establishing a way of life that is rich and responsive to the needs of body and soul is led by leaders who are willing to face their own human situation, to allow others to name their realities and then work from what's real rather than what they wish was real. "I'm experiencing dangerous levels of exhaustion." "The pace of our life in ministry is wearing me out." "I'm losing touch with spiritual reality because we're not taking time for rest, prayer and discernment." Statements like these can be made, challenged and grappled with in the presence of this kind of leader.

The process of crafting a life-giving way of life in community is led by leaders who are willing to make tough calls on concrete matters that affect our pace and our levels of expectation. Such decisions include (but are not limited to) adding services, building a new building and adding new ministry initiatives. When making such decisions spiritual leaders ask, "How will this decision affect our quality of life, the quality of our relationships in community, our families, our attention to prayer and spiritual journeying, our ability to maintain sane rhythms of work and rest (particularly the sabbath)?" Spiritual leaders think these thoughts, ask these questions, and initiate conversations and forums for addressing these issues in a proactive way, rather than assuming that people can figure such things out by themselves.

The process of establishing rhythms is led by leaders who are willing to move beyond privatized approaches to the spiritual life and proactively cultivate cultural norms that are transforming rather than deforming. Gary Haugen, president and CEO of the International Justice Mission (IJM) in Washington, D.C., is a leader who has been very intentional about establishing such rhythms in an organizational environment that is intensely activistic in its endeavors to promote justice and healing in areas where evil runs rampant. A human rights agency that secures justice for victims of slavery, sexual exploitation and other forms of violent oppression, IJM lawyers, investigators and aftercare professionals work tirelessly with local government officials to ensure immediate victim rescue and aftercare, to prosecute perpetrators, and to promote functioning public justice systems.

Gary, a former senior trial attorney for the U.S. Department of Justice, founded IJM in response to injustice that he witnessed in his work exposing and confronting human rights abuses in Africa. He began dreaming of and planning for IJM in 1994 while still working for the Department of Justice. Soon Gary left his position with the DOJ in order to devote himself wholly to this new endeavor. IJM became operational in 1997. When it became clear that IJM was going to take root and grow, he took a brief sabbatical. During that time he spent several hours a day in prayer, looking back over the previous years and asking God the simple question, "What was of you and what wasn't of you?" One of the things God spoke to him most clearly about was "prayer-less striving." Gary was deeply convicted about this and thought, *Let's just make sure we never go through a day without praying.*

What emerged was the establishment of IJM's first rhythm—an eleven o'clock prayer time during which the entire staff simply stopped their work and gathered to read a psalm and pray. At first it took only about fifteen minutes, but today it has evolved into a half-hour of prayer for the needs of the organization, those they are serving and the dangers they are facing.

I first connected with Gary when he wrote to me after the release of *Invitation to Solitude and Silence*. In a personal note he wrote, "I have given your book to all our employees and it has become an integral part of what we call '8:30 Stillness.' Everyone on our staff gets paid to be here early and to take 30 minutes (no phone, no email), to be still and silent with God each morning before going out to do his work of justice. Due in part to your accessible guidance, this time has been an encouraging and challenging blessing to us as a whole." Intrigued, I connected with Gary a couple of times over the next few years to learn more about what had taken place in his own spiritual life that moved him to take such a courageous step and to hear more about what it had been like for this group of active Christians to live into such rhythms together.

Gary told me that the idea for 8:30 Stillness came out of another sabbatical that he had taken several years later after IJM was up and running and, once again, he found himself exhausted and needing a word from the Lord. He came back from that sabbatical with the conviction that God wanted to pour out more of his power and presence on the ministry of IJM but that they were not spiritually ready to receive it. "I felt we needed a way of releasing what was cluttering our hands. We needed more of his power but we needed to be more spiritually prepared to receive it."

Out of that awareness and conviction, he instituted a rhythm of having the staff arrive at 8:30, but they did not open the doors or start work until 9:00. This time of stillness simply created space for individuals to spiritually prepare for the day, to look at what was coming down the pike for that day and talk to God about it, to allow whatever was underneath the surface to come forward—in whatever way was comfortable for each individual. "This rhythm invited very earnest, cerebral, action-oriented Christians to be still before God—which is not easy—but it is the right struggle."

The choice to be committed to spiritual rhythms in the context of the fast-paced, power-drenched environment of Washington, D.C., is radical by any standard. When I asked Gary what he notices about the impact of these rhythms on their lives personally and as an organization he mentioned three things: "Humility—because we discover that it is so difficult, even for us as Christians, to just be with God and that is very humbling! Wisdom—that does not necessarily come in the times of silence but comes in moments when you need it. There is a different kind of quiet inside for hearing God. And peace. The kinds of urgent, painful things we deal with on a daily basis can make us anxious and frustrated, but the practice of being quiet in God's presence brings us back to a place of trust in God." What church or organization doesn't need a little more of that?

THE NEW NORMAL

In a culture of spiritual transformation it becomes normative to take time for breathing, for prayer, for quiet at the beginning of important meetings and at important junctures during any meeting. It becomes normal for staff people to have a solitude day each month and normal for supervisors to talk about this with those who report to them. It is normal to take all vacation time and to be completely unplugged during that time; this may mean clearly communicated systems must be put in place to handle what is needed "back at the ranch." In such an environment it is normal to look at job descriptions and ask, "Is this realistic for one person in a normal work week? And what is a normal work week— forty hours, fifty hours? So they take two consecutive days off? When will they take a sabbath?"

The process of cultivating a life-giving way of life in community is led by leaders who make it a norm in their working relationships to listen deeply to each person's capacities, the demands of their job, what is realistic and sane given that person's stage of life, personality type, extenuating circumstances (a marriage that is struggling, a health crisis, caring for aging parents and the like).

My own rhythms these days seem relatively simple given how central they are to my ongoing ability to be engaged in ministry and how utterly essential they are to my well-being. My daily rhythm includes solitude and silence in the morning until nine o'clock. During this time I am unavailable by phone and do not check e-mail. My daily rhythms also include some form of exercise every day—alternating strength training with cardiovascular activities such as biking or walking. Often I am able to use my times of walking and biking for reviewing my day with God in order to celebrate the transformations that are taking place in my life and to allow him to reveal those places where I was subject to sin and negative patterns. I am also very clear on how much rest I need and view getting enough sleep and rest as an important part of my spiritual life.

Sunday is our sabbath as a family. We go to church early and the remainder of the day is spent in rest and delight. If I am traveling or preaching on a Sunday, I try to find another day in the week for additional rest even though Sundays are clearly optimal.

Extended times of silence before and after speaking engagements have become a routine part of my rhythm as well. As my speaking responsibilities have increased, I have also increased the time I spend in silence for all the reasons we explored earlier. Time spent in silence ahead of time is part of my preparation for speaking and time in silence afterward is part of my rest and recovery. I am also committed to a day a month in solitude (a bare minimum for people in ministry) and one extended retreat (two or more days) at least once a year. I have learned that retreat time is not the same thing as family vacation, and both are necessary.

There is something deeply spiritual about honoring the limitations of our existence as human beings—physical and spiritual creatures in a world of time and space. There is something about establishing rhythms that are gracious and accepting of our human limits that enables us to be gracious and accepting with others. There is an energy that comes from being rested that is different from the energy that comes from being driven. There is a wisdom that comes from silent listening that is different from what comes from talking things to death. There is right action that comes from waiting on God that is utterly different from reactivity. There is a renewed engagement in battle that is different from slogging through life with unremitting and stoic resolve. All of these rhythms create space for God, fostering an ability to bring something truer to the world than all of our doing. All of these rhythms put us in touch with something more real in ourselves and others than what we are all able to produce. We touch our very being in God.

Surely that is what the people around us need most.

PRACTICE

This chapter is not meant to be an exhaustive list of spiritual rhythms; rather it is meant to introduce the idea of rhythms in much the same way as the Israelites were introduced to the daily and weekly rhythms that would shape their lives (Exodus 16). It is also meant to highlight a few of the rhythms that are most significant for leaders as they seek a way of life for themselves that can eventually become so good and life giving that others want to emulate it and the community is strengthened. (For a more complete treatment of the subject of spiritual rhythms, see *Sacred Rhythms* by Ruth Haley Barton [Downers Grove, Ill.: InterVarsity Press, 2006].)

Use your time in solitude today to notice your own rhythms—or lack of them! You might consider the rhythms of solitude and community (an overarching theme of this book), work and rest (sabbath keeping), stillness and action, silence and word, engagement and retreat. How are these rhythms present in your life daily and weekly? How do you experience them nurturing and sustaining your physical life and your life in God? Allow this noticing to deepen your commitment to these life-giving rhythms.

What rhythms are missing for you, and what is the result of that in your life? Is there any rhythm in particular that you sense God inviting you to that corresponds to an area of concern or need? (For instance, if you are facing a major challenge that feels like an impasse, God may be inviting you to more stillness and a commitment not to act until you have heard from God. Or maybe your levels of depletion are of great concern to you and you realize that you do not keep a sabbath for yourself; God may be inviting you to incorporate this rhythm into your life as a pastor or ministry leader. Or maybe you are in the midst of a fierce conflict or battle and you realize that you have sustained injuries but have not taken time to retreat.)

Do not feel as if you have to add everything all at once. When you introduce even a couple of basic rhythms, the quality of your life and your leadership will begin to change for the better. This is not a problem-solving exercise to approach primarily with your mind. This is an opportunity to sit openly with God and pay attention to your life, to notice without judging, and to listen for how God might be leading you. Allow the following meditation to guide you into gratitude for God's goodness in building rhythms into the very nature of things. Let it help you touch your longing to enter into such rhythms.

■   ■   ■

Sabbath in Late Fall
For everything there is a season . . .

Sometimes on the Sabbath
all you can do is
    settle into the soft body of yourself
    and listen to what it says.
Listen to
    the exhaustion that is deeper than tiredness
    the hunger that is for more than food
    the thirst that is for more than drink
    the longing for comfort that is more than physical.

On the Sabbath
body and soul reach out for time of a different sort
    time that is full of space rather than activity:
    time to watch the burning bush in your own back yard . . .
    the movement of the wind among bare branches . . .
    the last leaf clinging to the branch before its final letting
    go.

Letting go is hard,
    letting go of that which no longer works
    that which no longer brings joy and meaning
    that which is no longer full of life.

It seems cruel
That something that used to be so beautiful
    should fall to the ground
    sinking into the earthy mud along with everything else that is
    dying,
    no longer recognizable for what it used to be.

It seems cruel but it is the way of things.

One generation gives its life for the next.

   One season slips away so another can come.

   One crop of fruit falls from the tree so that more can be borne.

   One wave recedes while another gathers strength to crash upon the shore.

It seems cruel

   but it is the rhythm of things.

   And rhythm has its own beauty.

RUTH HALEY BARTON, 2006

9

LEADERSHIP
AS INTERCESSION

The people cried out to Moses. . . .

So Moses prayed to the LORD.

EXODUS 17:3-4

A couple of years ago, our family watched a season of the reality TV show *Survivor* because we were acquainted with one of the participants—former NFL quarterback Gary Hogeboom. Gary emerged early on as a leader on his team—probably because of his age, his experiences on the football field and his responsibilities as a father of five children. After the season was over, an interviewer asked how he felt about it all. He responded, "I didn't want to be the leader, because the leader always gets voted off the island!"

Most of us who have been in leadership for any length of time at all can resonate with this statement. I have seen and experienced things in leadership for which I still don't have categories and may never this side of heaven. But one thing is sure: the choice to lead something, to orient your life toward some vision or ideal and to lead in that direction, opens you up to a world of pain that you might not otherwise have to face.

Gary's comment is an apt description of Moses' leadership experience as well. It seems the children of Israel were always trying to vote him off the island even though he had sacrificed everything to lead them! They were a particularly difficult group of people to work with. They complained a lot. They were headstrong. Sometimes they lied and were

> *A major difficulty in sustaining one's mission*
>
> *is that others who start out with the same enthusiasm*
>
> *will come to lose their nerve. Mutiny and sabotage*
>
> *come not from enemies who opposed the initial idea,*
>
> *but rather from colleagues whose will*
>
> *was sapped by unexpected hardships along the way.*
>
> EDWIN FRIEDMAN, *A FAILURE OF NERVE*

in other ways deceitful. They were rebellious and fickle. They were ungrateful and seemed to have a very short memory regarding all that God (and Moses!) had done for them. At times they even maneuvered behind Moses' back to oust him and appoint new leaders—one of the most painful things that can happen to a leader! Even his own brother and sister at one point questioned God's anointing on his life, succumbing to an insidious jealousy that nearly cost them their lives.

The Scriptures describe in great detail Moses' difficulties with the people he was leading, and it is one of the things I find most helpful about Moses' story. When people start to fix blame on the leader for all that is going wrong, the loneliness and disillusionment can be blinding. And yet this is one of the most predictable patterns we encounter in leadership. What is one to *do* with the people pains involved in leadership? How do we keep going when people turn against us and seek to undermine the very journey we have embarked upon together?

WHAT'S REALLY GOING ON

One of the basic disciplines that characterized Moses' life as a spiritual leader was his commitment to intercessory prayer, and it seemed to be essential to his ability to sustain himself in ministry and find the wisdom he needed. But in order to carry the people into God's presence with a pure heart and a real commitment to their well-being, he needed to understand what was really going on.

The late Edwin Friedman, in his work applying family systems theory to life in congregations, says that criticism of the leader (which is a form of sabotage) is so predictable that it should be viewed as part and parcel of the leadership process itself.

> Self-differentiated leadership always triggers sabotage which is a *systemic* part of leadership—so much so that a leader can never assume success merely because he or she had brought about change. It is only after having first brought about change and then sub-

sequently endured the resultant sabotage that the leader can feel truly successful. When the sabotage comes, this is the moment when the leader is most likely to experience a failure of nerve and seek a quick fix.

This is exactly what happened to Moses. He had gotten the people out of Egypt, which was a huge and highly beneficial change; but after the initial excitement, patterns of criticism and sabotage kicked in almost immediately. The people complained and began to talk about turning back when they hit their very first challenge—the Red Sea (Exodus 14). Then they added insult to injury by reminiscing about being in the land of Egypt, "when we sat by the fleshpots and ate our fill of bread." They accused Moses and Aaron of bringing them into the wilderness "to kill this whole assembly with hunger" (16:3).

This pattern of complaining and blaming the leader repeated itself with utter predictability throughout their journey, and Moses dealt with it in a couple of different ways. First of all, he refrained from taking it all too personally; he refused to accept responsibility for what was ultimately God's responsibility. Although he would not have had our modern-day jargon to discuss it, he seemed to have some understanding of the psychological process of projection—the way human beings unconsciously project their doubt and darkness onto someone else rather than taking responsibility for dealing with their own fear and anxiety. He might have also realized that people tend to project idealized expectations onto leaders—expectations that are often unspoken and held subconsciously—and then become angry when the leader does not meet those expectations.

But Moses refused to take on the weight of the Israelites' expectations. He would not allow them to treat him as if he were God nor behave as though he were responsible for something he was not. When they tried to put him in that larger-than-life role, he stopped it immediately by saying, "What are we, that you complain against us? When the LORD gives you meat to eat in the evening and your fill of bread in the morning . . . what are we? Your complaining is not against us but against the LORD" (Exodus 16:7-8). With one penetrating statement, Moses clarified the issue and shut down the projective process, insisting that they take it up with the One who was actually responsible.

It required a lot of discipline for Moses not to allow himself to get hooked into an argument, and I'm sure it was very hard to maintain at times, but the benefits were immeasurable. Not only did it relieve Moses of the burden of people's projections—a weight too heavy for any of us to carry—but is also freed him up to do what was most needed in the moment, which was to enter into the work of intercession. Unencumbered by the weight of undue responsibility, he was free to carry the people into God's presence and intercede on their behalf.

THE WORK OF INTERCESSION

One of the most consistent patterns of Moses' life in leadership is the regularity with which he prayed for the people he was leading and sought God's guidance for situations involving them. Rather than getting caught up in defending himself or arguing a point, he used his energy to carry the people into the presence of God, to cry out on their behalf and to listen to God for their next steps. Over and over again the pattern was very consistent: "The people complained . . . and Moses cried out to the LORD."

At Marah, when the people complained that they could not drink the water because it was bitter, Moses "cried out to the LORD" on their behalf (Exodus 15:23-25).

When they quarreled with Moses and with God at Rephidim, "Moses cried out to the LORD," asking God what to do (Exodus 17:3-4). Rather than lashing out at them or getting hooked into trying to prove himself to them, he battled it out in private with God.

When the people sinned by worshiping the golden calf, Moses' intercession saved them from being completely annihilated by God's anger.

"Moses implored the LORD. . . . And the LORD changed his mind" (Exodus 32:11, 14). Moses laid his life on the line and identified with the people completely as he interceded for them, saying, "If you will only forgive their sin—but if not, blot me out of the book that you have written" (Exodus 32:32).

When the people complained against God in the desert and the fire of the Lord burned against them, "Moses prayed to the LORD, and the fire abated" (Numbers 11:2).

When Miriam was afflicted with leprosy because she and Aaron had become jealous and challenged Moses' authority, "Moses cried to the LORD, 'O God, please heal her'" (Numbers 12:13).

When the people refused to believe God and enter boldly into the Promised Land, it got so bad that they threatened to displace Moses and Aaron and appoint new leaders, and God's anger burned against them. Once again, Moses interceded for the people, reminding God of his character and his covenant: "Forgive the iniquity of this people according to the greatness of your steadfast love," he prayed (Numbers 14:19).

When Korah led a revolt against Moses and the whole congregation assembled against him, which brought about a punishing plague, Moses and Aaron carried incense into the middle of the congregation to make atonement for them (Numbers 16:46-47). Moses literally "stood between the dead and the living; and the plague was stopped" (Numbers 16:48).

When God sent fiery serpents among the people because they had become impatient and spoke against God and Moses, Moses prayed for the people, and God instructed him to make an image of a serpent and set it on a pole so that everyone who had been bitten could look at it and live (Numbers 21:9).

Perhaps the story from Moses' life that most fully captures the significance of intercessory prayer as one of the basic functions of spiritual leadership is the battle with Amalek in Exodus 17. It is a picture that is worth a thousand words. Moses was no coward, and he was usually the front-line person when it came to the challenges that faced the Israelites on the journey, but in this case somehow he had a sense that his most important role in the battle was to stand on the top of a hill and intercede for the Israelite army. He appointed Joshua as general for this battle. "I will stand on the top of the hill," he promised, "with the staff of God in my hand" (Exodus 17:9)—a symbol of God's empowering presence and his reliance on God in his leadership.

We all know the story—whenever Moses held up his hands, Israel prevailed, and whenever he lowered his hands, Amalek prevailed. This work of interceding—seeking the presence of God on behalf of others— was so real and so taxing that Moses' hands grew weary. But he knew better than to engage in this ministry alone. He had brought with him Aaron and Hur (who, by the way, was the son of Caleb), two of his most trusted colleagues. They took a stone and put it under Moses to support him physically. Then they stood on each side of Moses and supported him with their presence, holding up his hands to keep them steady until the sun set. *This battle was literally won on the basis of Moses' ability to remain in a stance of intercessory prayer on behalf of those God had given him to lead.*

The number of times that Moses stood between the people and God interceding on their behalf and the impact that his intercessions had on the outcome of each situation are worth noting for their sheer magnitude! Clearly, for Moses, intercession was a significant function of spiritual leadership.

Being this reliant on God for the actual outcome of things is a very edgy way to lead. We are much more accustomed to relying partly on God and partly on our own plans and thoughts if the issues at hand are really important. "If you want to get the job done right, you better do it yourself!" is a sentiment that we apply not only to people but to God himself. It is always good to have a back-up plan if the life of faith doesn't come through, we rationalize. But Thomas Merton provides a perspective that has challenged me to walk right out to the edge of faith at key moments in my own life and leadership. He says,

Cowardice keeps us double minded—hesitating between the world and God. In this hesitation, there is no true faith—faith remains an opinion. We are never certain, because we never quite give in to the authority of an invisible God. This hesitation is the death of hope. We never let go of those visible supports which, we well know, must one day surely fail us. And this hesitation makes true prayer impossible—it never quite dares to ask for anything, or if it asks, it is so uncertain of being heard that in the very act of asking, it surreptitiously seeks by human prudence to construct a make-shift answer (cf. James 1:5-8).

What is the use of praying if at the very moment of prayer, we have so little confidence in God that we are busy planning our own kind of answer to our prayer?

THE POWER OF INTERCESSION

During Moses' times of intercession, God gave him specific guidance for how to stay faithful to his calling in the midst of whatever he was going through, and he usually emerged with specific guidance for the community. In fact, the people of Israel had come to look forward to receiving a word from the Lord through Moses with such anticipation that there was an entire ritual enacted around Moses' regular times of entering into God's presence.

There was a special place outside the camp called the tent of meeting, which was available to everyone who sought the Lord. But when Moses went to the tent of meeting, it was something of a national holiday.

Whenever Moses went out to the tent, all the people would rise and stand, each of them, at the entrance of their tents and watch Moses until he had gone into the tent. When Moses entered the tent, the pillar of cloud would descend and stand at the entrance of the tent, and the LORD would speak with Moses. When all the people saw the pillar of cloud standing at the entrance of the tent, all the people would rise and bow down, all of them, at the entrance of their tent. Thus the LORD used to speak to Moses face to face, as one speaks to a friend. (Exodus 33:8-11)

How it must have shaped the Israelite journey to experience this kind of awe and reverence when Moses entered into solitude to intercede for those he had been given to lead and love and to seek a word from the Lord. And how it must have shaped Moses himself!

The practice of intercessory prayer has been a hard one for me to incorporate into my life in leadership because the way it was taught to me early in my Christian experience made it so weighty and burdensome. It often involved elaborate lists for praying around the world (in thirty days or less), promises made ("I'll pray for you") that were very hard to keep, and thinking really hard about what to pray for (since clearly God wouldn't know what to do for the person I was praying for unless I told him!). And when it came to the difficult experiences in leadership— my first response to criticism, complaining, subtle jealousies and other kinds of bad behavior was generally *not* to pray for those who persecuted me or otherwise tried to vote me off the island. I had a variety of preferred responses ranging from fight to flight, and none of them included intercessory prayer!

However, a leader's own journey into solitude and silence can have a profound effect on the way we pray for others—or at least it has for me. As I have deepened my capacity to be with God with what is true about me and have learned more about how to wait for God's deliverance in my own life, it has not only changed my approach to praying for others but even changed my understanding of what intercessory prayer *is*. I realize now that intercessory prayer is not primarily about thinking that I know what someone else needs and trying to wrestle it from God. Rather, it is being present to God on another's behalf, listening for the prayer of the Holy Spirit that is already being prayed for that person before the throne of grace, and being willing to join God in that prayer.

Intercessory prayer is more about *not knowing* than it is about knowing. It is about growing more and more comfortable with the truth of Romans 8—that I do not know how to pray as I ought, for myself or anyone else, and accepting the fact that the Holy Spirit is the one who really knows how to pray and is *already* interceding for that person or that situation before the throne of grace. As I enter into the stillness of true prayer, it is enough to experience my own groaning about the situation or person I am concerned about and to sense the Spirit's groaning on their behalf.

The attitude of intercessory prayer is a willingness to enter into God's prayer in us, the caring love of God for ourselves, for others. In this place of prayer, we become sensitized to God's unique invitations to us as participants in that love, we may be called to let go of some of our vested interests and our traditional ways of caring for other people. Presence and absence, silence and words, doing and not doing all become relativized against the backdrop of God's prayer in us.

This has proved to be less burdensome than some of the ways I have done intercession in the past!

> *I look at God, I look at you, and I keep looking at God.*
>
> JULIAN OF NORWICH

I am also careful about how I use prayer lists. Now, as I sit quietly in God's presence daily, I see who God brings to mind and heart. As they come into my awareness, I invite them into that place where God's Spirit and my spirit are communing, and we sit together with that person. If I have a list or if there are people and concerns weighing on me, I bring those too, and we sit together with them. I don't feel burdened by the need to figure anything out or to say words that indicate that I somehow have a handle on the situation. It is enough to share the love, the rest and the care of God with them in this way.

If words do come or if there is something that I want to ask for, I certainly feel free to say this to God, but there is no pressure to do so. Most times there is nothing for me to do or say except to hold the people and situations that are of concern to me in God's presence and listen. Sometimes there will be some word of wisdom, some guidance, some action that God invites me to relative to that person or situation, but this is always something that is given—not something I have had to grasp for or work really hard to get.

If nothing comes, then I don't do or say anything—no matter how tempted I feel to assuage my anxiety by trying to make something happen. If the words aren't there, I don't say anything. If the words are there—perhaps God has brought me a Scripture, a word, an action or next step—then I seek to be faithful to what I have heard.

If someone asks me to pray for them, I promise them that I will do so *as God brings them to mind,* which leaves the responsibility in God's hands, not mine. As long as I am creating time and space to be in God's presence on behalf of others, I am confident that God, in his love, will bring those people to me during such times. Over time, this kind of intercessory prayer practice has been more peaceful and much less effortful than prayer practices that depend on considerable human thought and striving. And I am much more confident that I am actually allowing God to guide me into the prayers that are mine to pray.

ENTERING INTO THE SUFFERING OF GOD'S PEOPLE

I have also found that remaining attentive to my own search for God in the midst of my humanness has helped me become more comfortable with the humanness of others and less apt to make it my job to fix them. Being with the tenderness and vulnerability of my own humanity in

> *When my consciousness reaches up to God,*
>
> *and out to a person whom God loves,*
>
> *I yearn for them to be together. As I hold them together*
>
> *in my imagination, as I hold them in the orbit of my love,*
>
> *I am engaging in intercessory prayer.*
>
> GORDON COSBY, FOUNDING PASTOR, CHURCH OF THE SAVIOUR

God's presence teaches me how to be with others in the tenderness and vulnerability of their humanity.

Seeing and naming my own woundedness helps me know how to be with someone else as they are getting glimpses of their woundedness, and I am less compelled to meddle so much.

Staying in touch with the undercurrent of longing and desire in my own life helps me be reverent in the face of others' attempts to express their longing and desire.

Facing the great unfixables of my own life and learning to live with them openly in God's presence helps me be more compassionate when others give me a glimpse of the great unfixables of their lives, with much less need to advice-give, problem-solve or fix.

Seeking to stay faithful to hearing and following God's call in my own life has been the very best preparation for supporting and guiding others as they seek to say yes to God's risky invitations in their lives.

THE SOUL OF LEADERSHIP

There is a necessary transformation that takes place in the life of a leader as they experience their own sufferings and are changed by them *in relation to the people they lead*. A passage in Chaim Potok's novel *The Chosen* provides a powerful description of what this process is like. Near the

end of the book, Rabbi Reb Saunders speaks of his son Danny, whom
he had expected to follow in his footsteps and become a rabbi as well.
He says,

> When my Daniel was four, I realized that he was brilliant . . . but
> that there was no soul in my four-year-old Daniel, there was only
> his mind. He was a mind in a body without a soul. . . . I cried
> inside my heart, I went away and cried out to the Master of the
> Universe, "What have you done to me? A mind like this I need for
> a son? A *heart* I need for a son, a *soul* I need for a son, *compassion*
> I want from my son, righteousness, mercy, strength to suffer and
> carry pain, *that* I want from my son, not a mind without a soul!"

So Reb Saunders made the heart-wrenching choice to raise Danny
in almost complete silence—the way his father had raised him for the
purpose of preparing him to be a rabbi. He explained:

> My father himself never talked to me, except when we studied
> together. He taught me with silence. He taught me to look into
> myself, to find my own strength, to walk around inside myself
> in company with my own soul. When people would ask him why
> he was so silent with his own son he would say to them, . . . One
> learns of the pain of others by suffering one's own pain, he would
> say, by turning inside oneself, by finding one's own soul. And it is
> important to know of the pain, he said. It destroys our self-pride,
> our arrogance, our indifference toward others. . . . And when I was
> old enough to understand, he told me that of all people a tzaddik
> [spiritual leader] especially must know of pain. A tzaddik must
> know how to suffer for his people, he said. He must take their pain
> from them and carry it on his own shoulders. He must carry it al-
> ways. He must grow old before his years. He must cry, in his heart
> he must always cry. Even when he dances and sings, he must cry
> for the sufferings of his people.

By today's therapeutic standards this may sound a bit extreme, and some might take exception with how this is worded, but to do so would be to miss the point entirely. The point is that a leader is sensitized to the sufferings of his or her people by being in touch with his or her own suffering. It changes the way the leader carries them in his or her heart and in prayer.

There is no intellectual brilliance or strategic thinking or administrative excellence or gifted preaching that can make up for the ability to intercede for others in this way. This is the work of spiritual leadership.

As Henri Nouwen writes,

> A certain unavailability is essential for the spiritual life of the minister. . . . How would it sound when the question, "Can I speak to the minister" is not answered by "I'm sorry, he has someone in his office" but by "I'm sorry, s/he is praying." Could this not be a consoling ministry? What it says is that the minister is unavailable to me, not because s/he is more available to others, but because s/he is with God, and God alone—the God who is our God.

Who would we be if the practice of intercessory prayer shaped our leadership? How might it change the dynamic between us and those we are leading if they knew that we are regularly and routinely entering into God's presence with the intent to speak and lead from what transpires there?

PRACTICE

As you come to the end of this chapter, give yourself a few moments to breathe and become quiet in God's presence. Allow yourself the gift of enjoying the presence of God for your own soul's sake, and rest for a while in the familiarity and the intimacy of your friendship with God. Then, as you are ready, allow God to bring others to your heart and mind—any person or situation that is of concern to you, someone who has asked for your prayers, any person or group of persons who has been harsh or critical or complaining, any situation that is causing you stress or requires wisdom. Imagine God asking you, "Is it okay for us to invite this person to join us (*or for us to look at this situation together*)?"

If you are able to say yes, welcome that person into the space where you and God are communing, and be with that person (or situation) in God's presence. Listen for the prayer (the desire, the groaning) that the Holy Spirit is already praying for that person or situation before the throne of grace. Ask God, "How can I join you in that prayer?" See if there is anything God is inviting you to offer to that person or situation out of that prayer. Do not force or push for anything. If nothing comes, continue to rest in God relative to that situation. If wisdom or a next step does come, determine that you will respond faithfully as God makes your way clear.

If you notice resistance to inviting a person or situation into the time that you and God are sharing, feel free to tell God, "No, I'm not ready," and then pay attention to that together. Even your resistance can have a lot to tell you about what is really going on inside you relative to that person or situation.

It can be helpful to use written intercessory prayers that are designed to open up the space for others to be brought to mind. Such prayers can provide a way for us to hold our concerns in God's presence without having to work hard at it. These following intercessions are adapted from the *Iona Abbey Worship Book.*

Loving God, I hold in your healing presence those who suffer pain and ill health . . . (silence to allow the names and faces of those you know to come to mind, and then pray)
. . . May they know the deep peace of Christ.

Loving God, I hold in your healing presence those who suffer in mind and spirit . . .

. . . May they know the deep peace of Christ.

Loving God, I hold in your healing presence the suffering people of our world, and the places where people are experiencing hurt and division—including places of hurt and division in my own life . . .
. . . May we know the deep peace of Christ.

Loving God, I hold in your healing presence those experiencing grief and loss . . .
. . . May they know the deep peace of Christ.

Loving God, I hold in your healing presence those who need wisdom for their next steps . . .
. . . May they know the deep peace of Christ.

Loving God, I hold in your healing presence those people and situations that seem broken beyond repair . . .
. . . May they know the deep peace of Christ.

Loving God, I hold in your healing presence and peace those whose needs are not known to me but who are known by you, and those for whom I have been asked to pray . . .
And I name in my heart all those who are close to me . . .
. . . May they know the deep peace of Christ.

Glory to God, from whom all love flows,
glory to Jesus, who showed his love through suffering,
and glory to the Holy Spirit,
who brings light to the darkest places.
Amen.

IONA ABBEY WORSHIP BOOK

10

THE LONELINESS
OF LEADERSHIP

See, you have said to me,

"Bring up this people";

but you have not let me know

whom you will send with me. . . .

If your presence will not go,

do not carry us up from here.

EXODUS 33:12, 15

Leadership involves a very peculiar kind of loneliness. It has to do with seeing something that others do not see, do not see as clearly or perhaps have lost sight of. It involves staying faithful to God and to the tasks and decisions that are consistent with the journey God is leading us on even in the face of criticism, disbelief and failure. Those who began the journey with enthusiasm start to tire of the rigors of the journey. The water is bitter, the food is bad, the dangers unexpected. They start to long for the security and predictability of life as they knew it before, and they may begin to doubt whether the Promised Land exists anywhere but in the leader's imagination. They begin to entertain ideas about going back. "For it would have been better for us to serve the Egyptians than to die in the wilderness," they say (Exodus 14:12). Some days you are tempted to agree with them, but you know deep in your soul that even if others turn back you cannot.

It is one thing to put yourself in service of someone else's vision; it is quite another to have seen a vision yourself and know to the bottom of your being that you will go on and you must go on regardless of the choices that other people make. The loneliness of leadership is knowing that the buck stops here—there is something that has been given by God for you to do, and to renege would make you like Jonah hiding out in the bottom of the boat trying to pretend that he had not received a call from God. You could do it, but it wouldn't leave you with much of a life!

LONELY FOR GOD

Most of the time Moses seemed to take the struggles and difficulties of leadership in stride. He could deal with angry pharaohs and threatening armies. He could endure hunger and thirst. He could cope with harsh conditions and separation from his family. But there were times when the realization of *how alone he was in it all* was more than he could bear. The first time the loneliness of leadership became too much for him is recounted in Exodus 33, immediately after the people rebel against God and against Moses by worshiping the golden calf.

Moses had been on Mount Horeb waiting for a word from the Lord on behalf of the people. It took longer than anyone expected, but finally he descended from the mountain carrying stone tablets that contained the Ten Commandments, written by the very hand of God. This should have been a moment of great spiritual significance and celebration, but as he entered the camp he found that the people's tolerance for waiting had run out and they had turned to other gods. The worst part was that Aaron, his brother and right-hand man whom he had left in charge, had allowed the people to coerce him into this betrayal.

It is not hard to imagine the disappointment and disillusionment that Moses must have experienced as he surveyed the situation. It probably took every ounce of his strength to lead through the events of the next few days, as he literally stood between an angry God and a wayward people and tried to make atonement for their sins. Alone in God's presence, he begged God to be merciful, and his identification with his people was total. When it seemed that all was lost, he was willing to sacrifice his own life if it would placate an angry God. Putting his whole self on the line, he said, "But now, if you will only forgive their sin—but if not, blot me out of the book that you have written" (Exodus 32:32).

God and Moses fought it out one more time, and God did spare the people from being destroyed by his righteous anger. But the whole interaction took tremendous spiritual stamina on Moses' part, and when it was all over, he was wiped out. Not only were the people impossible to deal with, but God had informed Moses that he was still so angry that he would not be among them as they entered into the Promised Land. Even though he would continue to do certain things for them (like sending an angel to drive out the Canaanites), the bottom line was "I will not go up among you, or I would consume you on the way, for you are a stiff-necked people" (Exodus 33:3).

> *Moses was the greatest legislator and commander-in-chief*
>
> *of the first liberation army. He was a prophet,*
>
> *God's representative to the people and the people's*
>
> *representative to God. And he never*
>
> *had a good day in his life. Either the people were*
>
> *against him or God was against him.*
>
> ELIE WIESEL

IF YOUR PRESENCE WILL NOT GO

There is loneliness and then there is *loneliness*. What Moses encountered here was the deepest kind of loneliness—the loneliness of feeling abandoned by God. It was the emptiness of losing the one thing that mattered the most, the one thing that gave this journey its very meaning, and Moses was quite sure that he couldn't go on without *that*. So he just stopped. He refused to accept that God wanted to bail on the Israelite mission or supervise it from a distance, and he took it up with God directly, as he always did.

He said, "See, you have said to me, 'Bring up this people'; but you have not let me know whom you will send with me. Yet you have said, 'I know you by name, and you have also found favor in my sight.' Now if I have found favor in your sight, show me your ways, so that I may know you and find favor in your sight. Consider too that this nation is your people."

God responded, "My presence will go with you, and I will give you rest."

But Moses was not completely convinced. He wanted to make sure that God knew that he had reached a limit. "If your presence will not

> *I am told God loves me—and yet the reality of darkness*
>
> *and coldness and emptiness is so great that*
>
> *nothing touches my soul. . . . What tortures of loneliness . . .*
>
> *I wonder how long will my heart suffer like this?*
>
> MOTHER TERESA, *COME BE MY LIGHT*

go, do not carry us up from here. For how shall it be known that I have found favor in your sight, I and your people, unless you go with us? In this way, we shall be distinct" (Exodus 33:12-16).

Moses did have a point. How else would people know that they had found favor in God's sight if God's presence was not palpable among them? What was the point of continuing on if there was nothing to distinguish them from all the other nations that they passed through? But Moses needed more than just wordy assurances. He was desperate for a sign of God's favor—some assurance that he was not alone—and so he asked God to show him his glory. Who wouldn't want to see God's glory, after all?

But God knew that what Moses really needed was the assurance of God's goodness. Moses was well acquainted with God's justice, his power and his righteousness, and he had seen more than enough of God's anger and punishment. What he needed now was an experience of God's goodness, his graciousness and mercy. All of a sudden this was more important to him than any promised land he had ever dreamed of.

A LEADER'S GREATEST NEED

This is a pivotal moment in the life of a leader. It is the moment when whatever the promised land is for us—a church of a certain size, a new ministry, a new building, writing a book, being sought out as an expert—pales in significance when compared with our desire for God. At this point we might realize that we are missing the presence of God for ourselves personally. We might look around at what we've done or built and wonder whether we have gotten where we are merely through our own effort and whether we have somehow gotten out ahead of the very Presence that called us to this journey in the first place. Or maybe we see that our own relationship with God has been overtaken with ministry concerns, and we grieve the loss of a sense of God's presence deep within.

Leadership has taken a toll. A great emptiness has opened up, and we realize, as Moses did, that there is no promised land we could ever envision that matters nearly as much as the presence of God in our life right here and right now. Future possibilities are not enough, because we're not even sure we will be around to see them. It is no longer enough to know that others are experiencing the goodness of God *through* us; there has to be some goodness in it *for* us, something to sustain our own fragile soul.

I know this place because I have been there. It was during a season of many changes in our organization, and nothing about the journey was turning out the way I had expected. Although our ministry had proved to be effective in the lives of those we were serving, we continued to struggle to find a financial model that worked. Friends and colleagues whom we thought would be with us for the long haul were called to other places and priorities, and although we affirmed the rightness of their choices, the losses were great. Those of us who remained were working other jobs to generate income for our families while trying to remain faithful to the ministry we had been given in the time left over. Doing double duty made it difficult to sustain rhythms that were life giving for us, and we were truly exhausted. Even though we longed to give our best to the work we had been called to, most days we felt as if we weren't giving ourselves fully and effectively to anything. In addition, we had experienced an unexpected conflict that left us depleted and disillusioned. On more than one occasion I had been accused of being too idealistic, and the truth is, I was starting to wonder if my critics might be right. Taking a simple job at the department store on the corner was looking better and better!

During this time I came to a point where I was no longer sure if God was with me and with us, and I did not want to go any further without that Presence. I needed to experience God's goodness to me and to us in the midst of it all, and Moses' need for reassurance resonated deeply and consistently with my own need. My questions to God were similar to Moses', and Moses' story gave me permission to stop for a while so that I (and we) could ask them. Have we found favor in your sight, or is this just a product of our own striving and willfulness? What is the difference between willfulness and perseverance? And how does one know that a particular venture has found favor in God's sight—really? Is it about numbers? Is it about financial profitability or at least sustainability? Is it about personal comfort and ease? I did not want to be stubborn and willful, continuing to push something God was not blessing, but I also didn't want to give up if God was still in it and calling us forward.

I didn't know much, but what I did know was that I wasn't willing to go any farther without a sense of God's presence. I desperately needed to know that God was good—not just as a general characteristic of his person but that he was good *toward me*. As scary as it was to admit it, I was willing to stop the whole operation if I didn't have some assurance of God's favor and God's presence.

THE INWARD JOURNEY

When we begin to experience this kind of existential loneliness, no trite answers or superficial responses will do. One more accomplishment or achievement or title or degree after our name will not satisfy our need—and the only reason we know that is because we have tried it all. Something *is* missing, and that missing thing is the experience of the presence of God that we felt so strongly when we began and that has now become a distant memory.

This kind of loneliness must drive us first and foremost to God, because there is no one else and nothing else that can answer such a deep heart cry. Recognizing and accepting this kind of aloneness for what it is prevents us from being seduced into believing that our restlessness can be satiated "out there" in the realm of activity, success, notoriety and social connections. This in itself is no small thing, for allowing ourselves to face our ultimate aloneness compels us to "travel *inward*," as Moses did, "to meet ourselves and to meet the infinite love and riches of God dwelling inside our beings." Then, and only then, can our loneliness be transformed into a fruitful solitude in which the fullness of God's presence fills all emptiness.

It takes courage to face our loneliness, to ask God for what we need and to wait for God's response as Moses did. And God finally met Moses in the place of his deepest need. He said, "I will do the very thing that you have asked; for you have found favor in my sight, and I know you by name." Then Moses made his request, a request that reflected what he thought he needed. He asked to see God's glory, but God knew better. God knew that what Moses most needed to see and what would sustain him for the long haul of leadership was a glimpse of God's goodness and mercy. "I will make all my goodness pass before you, and will proclaim before you the name, 'The LORD'; and I will be gracious to whom I will be gracious, and will show mercy on whom I will show mercy" (Exodus 33:17-19).

God's goodness is his greatest glory and it is what we most need. One more time and in one more way, God was letting Moses know that he had chosen Moses to be the recipient of God's goodness and grace. But even with the privileged relationship that God and Moses shared, "all God's goodness" would be too much for any mere mortal to bear—even Moses. So God invited Moses to come closer, to "a place by me where you shall stand on the rock; and while my glory passes by I will put you in a cleft of the rock, and I will cover you with my hand until I have passed by" (Exodus 33:21-22).

We do not know exactly what this moment was like for Moses. Like the intimacies that pass between a husband and wife and cannot be fully disclosed without violating the sacredness of it, we do not know exactly what passed between Moses and God in this moment. But what we do know is that Moses emerged a changed person, one who was ready once again to take up the mantle of leadership and finish his race. Solitude became a place of encounter with God that led first to personal worship and then to an ability to mediate the very nature and presence of God to the people.

Moses' willingness to enter into solitude and face his aloneness was *not* merely for his own benefit. It was fruitful for himself and the people he was leading. God restored what had been lost (the stone tablets with the Ten Commandments), he showed Moses his goodness and his steadfast love in a way that he would never forget, and he established a covenant with Moses and the people. Moses emerged from solitude knowing what he needed to know to remain faithful to his calling, and his face shone with the knowledge of it.

Reassured by Moses' example, I stayed in Exodus 33 for a very long time. And in fact, our entire leadership community stayed in that place for a year. We cut back significantly on our ministry activities, asking God to show us in some unmistakable way that he was with us in this endeavor and that he wanted us to go on. We set a date for the board meeting at which we would decide whether God was calling us to continue. This was a very hard time—a season of not knowing—but in a strange way it was also a time of great freedom—the freedom that comes when we are truly willing to let go and are utterly given over to the will of God. If we did receive an indication of God's favor, we would go on. If we did not receive some clear indication of God's favor, we were willing to stop. It was a kind of surrender that was purifying in its effect.

Eventually, God did show us his goodness in a very concrete way. A foundation that had supported us in the past gave us a grant that enabled us to hire the administrative help that we desperately needed in order to function at the level our ministry now required. This financial gift met such a deep and practical need relative to our well-being that we experienced it immediately as an expression of God's goodness to us. In addition, the foundation gave us a matching grant that was intended specifically to help us develop our donor base—something that would benefit us over the long haul. We were not at our strongest point, and we knew that it was highly unusual for a foundation to be this generous given the state we were in. Their generosity was clearly God's gift to us in answer to the questions we were asking. When the foundation's representative informed me of the grants and said to me, "We believe in the importance of what you are doing, and we want you to survive," I took that as a word from the Lord, and it was in reliance on God's goodness that we took our next steps.

Since then I have not wondered in the same way whether God is with us or intended us to go on. That moment has become a touchstone for me relative to this particular ministry; since then, whenever I find myself doubting God's favor, I am able to remember that time of waiting and crying out to God. I am reminded of how God met us in the place of our questioning and something settles inside me once again.

STRENGTHENED IN THE INWARD BEING

Any leader who cannot endure profound levels of loneliness will not last long. None of us are immune to this intensely personal and yet utterly universal experience. In his book *A Failure of Nerve: Leadership in the Age of the Quick Fix,* Edwin Friedman identifies characteristics that are essential for all those who are leading toward something that is genuinely new. One is a willingness to be exposed and vulnerable relative to our fear of being alone. He says,

> One of the major limitations of imagination's fruits is the fear of standing out. It is more than the fear of criticism. It is anxiety at

being alone, of being in a position where one can rely little on others, a position that puts one's resources to the test, a position where one will have to take total responsibility for one's own response. Leaders must not only not be afraid of that position; they must come to love it.

This kind of loneliness—being in a position where we must take total responsibility for ourselves and for what God is calling us to do no matter what others are doing—is an absolute truth of leadership. None of us escapes it. Of course, this presents us with a real dilemma when we realize that no matter what the people around us are saying, no matter how much they are wishing to go back, the vision we have seen is so *real* that it is impossible for us to go back and live as we once did. There is a point where we have gotten so far away from Egypt, so far from a life lived in bondage, that we could not go back even if we wanted to. Even though the promised land is still far off, we have tasted enough of the dream to know that to go back would make us crazier than continuing to move forward. And even if we did go back, we probably would not get a very warm welcome!

> *It is easier to belong to a group than to belong to God.*
>
> RICHARD ROHR, *EVERYTHING BELONGS*

The way we can learn to love our aloneness, or at least to be at home in it, is to find God there as Moses did. This is a pivotal moment in the life of any leader. Martin Luther King Jr. tells the story of his own Exodus 33 moment in a sermon titled "Our God Is Able."

After the Montgomery bus protest had been undertaken, we began to receive threatening phone calls and letters. . . . At first I took them in my stride. . . . But as the weeks passed, I realized that many of the threats were in earnest. I felt myself . . . growing in fear.

After a particularly strenuous day, I settled in bed at a late hour . . . when the telephone rang. An angry voice said, "Listen, nigger, we've taken all we want from you. Before next week you'll be sorry you ever came to Montgomery." . . . I could not sleep. It seemed that all my fears had come down on me at once. . . .

I was ready to give up. . . . In this state of exhaustion, when my courage had almost gone, I determined to take my problem to God. . . . I bowed . . . and prayed aloud. . . . "I am here taking a stand for what I believe is right but now I am afraid. The people are looking to me for leadership, and if I stand before them without strength and courage, they too will falter. I am at the end of my powers. . . . I've come to the point where I can't face it alone."

At that moment I experienced the presence of the Divine as I had never before experienced him. It seemed as though I heard . . . an inner voice, saying, "Stand up for righteousness, stand up for truth. God will be at your side forever." Almost at once my fears began to pass from me. . . . The outer situation remained the same, but God had given me inner calm.

Three nights later, our home was bombed. Strangely enough, I accepted the word of the bombing calmly. *My experience with God* had given me new strength and trust. I knew now that God is able to give us the interior resources to face the storms . . . of life.

Have you ever come to a moment like this—when you knew that you could not continue to face the challenges of leadership alone, without some knowledge of God's goodness that you could be sure of? Have you ever had a moment when you realized that all that had gone before— past successes, past achievements, past experiences of God—meant nothing? A moment when loneliness and disillusionment were so deep that nothing out there in the future—no carrot dangling on the end of a stick—could make the sacrifice seem worth it? A moment when you realized that none of the trappings of leadership—no role, no title, no accomplishment, no vision for some future reality—could touch the emptiness on the inside and you were ready to stop if you did not know for sure that God was with you? Are you there right now?

If your answer is yes, thank God for it, because this may be the moment of your greatest freedom—freedom from being so driven by visions of future possibilities that you are distracted from seeking God in the here and now. Thank God for it, because this is the moment when you *know* down to the bottom of your being that the nearness of God is your ultimate good and you are not willing to go on without it. Thank God for it, because now you know that you are no longer willing to sacrifice intimacy with God for anything—even the promised land you have envisioned. Thank God because the goodness of the Lord—which fills all emptiness—is about to pass by.

------------------------------ **PRACTICE** ------------------------------

Take time to be with God with your own loneliness of leadership. Notice which kind of loneliness seems to be most prevalent for you right now— the loneliness that comes from criticism and sabotage, the loneliness of being alienated and estranged from meaningful human connection, the loneliness of feeling disconnected or abandoned by God, the loneliness of carrying too much of the burden alone. Using the following prayer (if it seems appropriate), simply open up your loneliness to God and allow him to meet you in that place. If you can, you might even thank God for the way your loneliness keeps you relentlessly seeking after him.

■　■　■

Blessed are you
who has given each man a shield of loneliness
so that he cannot forget you.

You are the truth of loneliness,
and only your name addresses it.

Strengthen my loneliness
that I may be healed in your name,
which is beyond all consolations
that are uttered on this earth.

Only in your name
can I stand in the rush of time,
only when this loneliness is yours
can I lift my sins toward your mercy.

LEONARD COHEN, *BOOK OF MERCY*

11

FROM ISOLATION
TO LEADERSHIP
COMMUNITY

I am not able to carry all this people alone,

for they are too heavy for me.

NUMBERS 11:14

To really grapple with our loneliness in God's presence as Moses did is no small thing. Our loneliness calls us to move more deeply into the realm of faith, where we discover that there is a Presence who is the ultimate fulfillment of our emptiness and who grounds us in what is real and unchanging. But there is another kind of loneliness that plagues us: the isolation that comes from carrying too much of the burden alone and not having a safe place for our own soul. Moses faced this kind loneliness in Numbers 11. The people were complaining once again, and "the rabble among them" (v. 4) had whipped everyone into a frenzy of discontent. Even with the adjustments he had made earlier to spread out the workload and in spite of his intimacy with God, Moses came to the end of himself once again, and this time he didn't need anyone else to point it out. This time he knew it himself.

The cumulative effect of carrying the burden alone was taking its toll. He had been leading the Israelites for such a long time, and the job was much bigger than it used to be. The people now numbered 600,000—a significantly larger group than most of us will ever lead! They were once again complaining about the rigors of the journey. God was providing manna daily, but a group of malcontents had a strong craving for meat and stoked everyone else's dissatisfaction with their complaining. Whole families were standing in the entrances of their tents weeping. God was angry at the people, and Moses was angry at God. The burden of leadership had become too much, and Moses did what he always did: he went marching into God's presence to tell him that he just could not go on this way.

At first he blustered, accusing God of giving him more than he could bear. He even resorted to throwing out cynical rhetorical questions. "Did I give birth to them, that you should say to me, 'Carry them in your bosom, as a nurse carries a sucking child?' " (v. 12). But cynicism and anger were just a cover for the more tender emotions of sadness, despair and loneliness. Eventually Moses got to the heart of his frustration and despair and said, I give up. "I am not able to carry all this people alone, for they are too heavy for me. If this is the way you are going to treat me, put me to death at once" (vv. 14-15).

This was an extreme statement, to be sure, but it brims with such unedited honesty and truth that one has to at least admire Moses for saying it. And it definitely took the conversation where it needed to go. Moses' ability to be honest about his desolation brought him to the end of his *self*-reliance, which in turn opened up space for God to be at work.

A Paradox of Leadership

Oftentimes a leader's soul is not strengthened in the community of those she or he is leading. In fact, life in the community of those one is leading often challenges and at times weakens the soul, as Moses' story so honestly depicts. There seemed to be no limit to the people's accusations and debilitating complaints, and the cumulative effect was very hard on his soul. He may even have found ways to keep himself somewhat aloof to shield himself from their projections, dissatisfaction and anger.

Moses was experiencing one of the great paradoxes of leadership: that we can be surrounded by people and be very busy doing good things and yet feel deeply alone with the burdens we bear. Over time the loneliness of decision-making, of being responsible for other people's well-being, ensuring adequate resources, staying faithful to a calling that seems impossible, wears us down. The irony is that by now we have learned how to wax eloquent about the idea of community, how to cast vision for it and how to help others experience it(!), but we have lost it for ourselves.

Oftentimes our feelings of isolation increase right along with our success. There are many reasons for this—some that have to do with the dynamics that others bring and some that have to do with ourselves. We might feel that our need for others is a sign of weakness that is incongruent with the in-control, I've-got-it-all-figured-out kind of person we think a leader is supposed to be. As the stakes get higher, we might find ourselves operating more and more out of the belief that if we want anything to be done right, we have to do it ourselves. We may have had enough hard knocks in relationships that we are no longer willing to trust ourselves in the deepest ways to anyone. To make matters worse, we might be so emotionally depleted that we don't cultivate community with other leaders, because *that* takes more energy than maintaining a purely professional relationship. And it's a whole lot less risky!

Whatever the reasons, this kind of isolation is a dangerous place for the leader to be. One day we wake up and realize that we are so empty inside that we want to die, or at least quit. Henri Nouwen describes his experience this way:

> After 25 years of priesthood, I found myself praying poorly, living somewhat isolated from other people and very much preoccupied with burning issues. Everyone was saying I was doing really well, but something inside was telling me that my success was putting my own soul in danger. . . . I woke up one day with the realization that I was living in a very dark place and that the term "burnout" was a convenient psychological translation for a spiritual death.

Clearly this moment in a leader's life is something of a crisis. In Moses' case God responded quickly with a plan. He told Moses to convene a gathering of the most respected elders in Israel, those who were trustworthy enough to come alongside Moses in his fragile condition, so they could talk about it together. The answer to Moses' desperate exhaustion and debilitating isolation was that God would take some of Moses' spirit and pour it out upon other trusted leaders so that they could carry the load together.

> Gather for me seventy of the elders of Israel, whom you know to
> be the elders of the people and officers over them; bring them to

the tent of meeting, and have them take their place there with you. I will come down and talk with you there; and I will take some of the spirit that is on you and put it on them; and they shall bear the burden of the people along with you so that you will not bear it all by yourself. (Numbers 11:16)

Whereas the previous restructuring seems to have been primarily organizational, God's instructions now addressed the extreme isolation Moses was experiencing at the soul level. It was his inner, psychic aloneness that God was seeking to alleviate by empowering a spiritual community of leaders to bear the emotional and spiritual burdens of leading the people. Again, the caliber of those selected was of utmost importance. These leaders needed to be those who had already committed themselves to the journey and who were fully vested in the vision. These were individuals who were already exercising spiritual leadership and were willing to wait with Moses for a visitation from the Lord. They were willing to go one step further in their leadership and actually receive some of the spirit that was on Moses.

A SHARED SPIRIT

What a stirring moment it must have been for Moses and for the individuals who gathered around the tent of meeting as God literally took part of the spirit of Moses and placed it on them. One of the ways they knew it was real was that they all prophesied—which had never happened before. It was proof that this "sharing of the spirit" was more than just rhetoric. Now they, too, bore the passion and responsibility for leading the people on this journey. By God's grace, Moses was no longer alone with all that he was carrying, and others now had the privilege of sharing more deeply in it. What a soul-strengthening experience this must have been!

When we get to the place, as Moses did, where our loneliness has become destructive, it is usually so deep that we cannot find our way out by ourselves. No trite answers or superficial responses will do. No mere

> *We only come into inner authority*
>
> *insofar as we admit a positive and mature*
>
> *dependency on others and freely*
>
> *enter into a mature exchange*
>
> *of life and power.*
>
> RICHARD ROHR, "AUTHORS OF LIFE TOGETHER"

organizational tweak will address this kind of isolation. We might have tried to assuage our loneliness or distract ourselves from it in various ways, but now we have no other option except to pour out our loneliness in God's presence and cast our very human self on his mercy.

During this time it is very important that we resist the urge to cling or to grasp unwisely at those who may or may not have the spirit to walk with us. This is a grave temptation that we indulge to our own peril. But by carrying our loneliness into the solitary place first, we encounter the caring presence of God, who hears our cry, and we open ourselves to receive those whom God is giving to bear the burden with us. These we watch for and welcome as a gift from God, so that together we can be open to God's life-giving Spirit among us.

BEYOND TEAMWORK

When God brings these partners, it is good to have some idea of what to do with them! This is more than an invitation to be part of a winning team. This is an invitation to spiritual community at the leadership level.

Those of us who were in the work force in the 1970s and 1980s were inspired—and rightly so—by the concept of teams and the wisdom of teams. If, like me, you have had the privilege of living in an area that boasts an award-winning sports team (like the Chicago Bulls in their hey-day), you know that effective teamwork yields great entertainment and great results! But as satisfying as teamwork can be, spiritual people who come together to lead churches or organizations with a spiritual purpose have a deeper calling—we are called to move beyond teamwork to spiritual community and to have our leadership emerge from that place.

A team gathers around a task, and when the task is over the team disbands. Spiritual community, on the other hand, is a much more permanent thing, because spiritual community gathers around a Person. In Moses' day, the community gathered around the presence of God as they experienced that Presence in the cloud and the fire; as New Testament believers, we gather around Christ, who is present to us through the Holy Spirit.

Jesus himself, when he was here on this earth to do God's will, did not create a high-performance team to get the job done. He did not put together a high-powered board or complex organization. Nor did he even choose the most strategic individuals from a human point of view! He chose a few individuals "whom he wanted," the Scriptures say (Mark 3:13), and he chose them first and foremost to be with him and, by virtue of their relationship with him, to be present with each other. Out of that togetherness and without much of a strategy, they changed the world.

Spiritual community is not something that we ourselves create. In his classic work *Life Together,* Dietrich Bonhoeffer points out, "Christian community is founded solely on Jesus Christ and in fact, it already exists in Christ. It is *not* an ideal which we must realize, it is rather a reality created by God in Christ *in which we may participate.* It is a spiritual and not a psychic reality in that it is created by the Spirit."

Moses did not create the leadership community that was birthed by the Spirit of God on that day when he was at the end of his rope, and neither do we. If we are confused on this point and think that it is somehow our responsibility to create community, then the burden will surely be more than we can bear. However, if we understand that we are invited to participate—to find ways to live into—this great reality called spiritual community, then we can embrace the values that undergird community. We can choose to establish practices that transform us in community. Spiritual community at the leadership level then becomes the context for discerning and doing the will of God, which is the heart of spiritual leadership.

VALUES THAT UNDERGIRD COMMUNITY

It is much easier to talk about community, and even try to create community for others, than it is to actually live it at the leadership level. Experiencing spiritual community at the leadership level is one of richest and most satisfying aspects of leadership, but it can also be one of the trickiest. The truth is, we are not very good at cultivating community when we get together to lead something. Somehow when we get into leadership settings we are much more prone to posturing and maneuvering and working the system. When our feathers get ruffled, we are better at creating lines of division, voting each other off the island or leaving each other when we can't find a way to come together in unity. Sometimes we even lob lawsuits at each other, subjecting spiritual community to a secular court system that has little understanding of the values and commitments associated with Christian community. This is a move that is expressly forbidden in New Testament Scripture and yet it is what we have learned to do.

Clearly, spiritual community among leaders does not happen by accident, nor is it maintained and cultivated in a haphazard way. It is led by leaders who are clear that this is what they are called to, who are committed to the values that undergird it and who are willing to guide others in living out community values in concrete ways. In order to experience spiritual community at the leadership level, the leadership group will need to live into its own experience of the values that will shape their life together and then learn to articulate those values in ways that are compelling for them.

One mistake we often make in a leadership setting is making too many assumptions about how we all approach community and what it means to each of us. If we assume that we all have the same ideas about it, we might stop short of actually developing a covenant or a set of clearly articulated commitments that we can all agree to. Then when difficulties or disagreements arise, we lack a set of guiding principles to inform our process of working through them.

Some values are very general, appropriate for any Christian church or organization; others will be more specific to the unique calling of that a particular community. Gordon Cosby, founding pastor of Church of the Saviour in the heart of Washington, D.C., observes this about their process of developing a covenant: "The written commitment has grown out of our life together. The life occurred first and then it was put down in a written commitment. To make a formal commitment without having drunk deeply of the life of the group is simply to take a husk that can mock us. Only in commitment can there be real belonging."

There are, of course, some values that are foundational for any group that calls itself Christian, but ultimately each leadership group will need to identify and articulate its own values that are biblically sound, relationally healthy, spiritually enlivening and meaningfully expressed in its context. As an example, here are a few that have been foundational in shaping our life in community over the years:

Community: We affirm that we are in our very essence a spiritual community gathered around the presence of Christ. *What we do* flows out of *who we are* in Christ. Learning to come together and stay together in unity is our first and most enduring task as we pattern our relationships after Christ's relationships with his disciples. "He loved [his own] to the end" (John 13:1; John 15 and 17). To compromise community would be to compromise our essence and then we would not have much that is of value to offer to others.

Spiritual Transformation: Each of us as individuals is committed to personal spiritual disciplines and to spiritual disciplines in community that support and catalyze our own spiritual transformation. It is routine for us to check in with each other about our spiritual rhythms when we are sharing privately or as a group. It is routine for us to talk about our pace of life and whether it is enabling us to remain healthy or whether we are approaching dangerous levels of exhaustion. It is routine for us to make scheduling decisions as a ministry organization on the basis of this kind of awareness and discussion.

Lived Experience: We agree that we will not teach theories or wishful thinking; we will teach only that which we are experiencing ourselves to some degree. "We speak of what we know and testify to what we have seen" (John 3:11). Sometimes this means that we choose not to teach on certain topics—even if it would be a great topic!—because we know we are not yet living them effectively.

Discernment: We are committed to the habit of discernment—seeking to be attentive and alert to God's activity among us day by day—and naming that together so that we can seek to respond faithfully. We are also committed to the practice of discernment—proactively seeking God's guidance together when we need specific direction for decision-making. Because discernment takes more time and a different kind of attention than decision-making, living out this value takes real discipline. [See chapter twelve for a more complete treatment of this.]

Truth-Telling: We believe that all truth, no matter how delicate or painful or seemingly inconsequential, contributes to the discernment process. God desires truth in the inward being because truth leads to freedom, spiritual transformation, and deeper levels of discernment. Since the Holy Spirit has been given to us to guide us into truth, we seek to offer the truth in love and gentleness rather than hiding truth or "spinning" the truth; anything less than this kind of honesty places the community in great peril as we know from the story of Ananias and Sapphira in Acts 5. Because we know this is such a deeply held value, it guides us and gives us courage to go ahead and say the hard thing and support each other in doing so.

Celebration: We believe that celebration is the spiritual discipline associated with gratitude. Thus, we look for every opportunity to celebrate God's presence with us and his activity among us. Our retreats always have one evening that is specifically designed for celebration.

Kindness: Kindness is a basic characteristic of mature spirituality but often the Christian community is unkind. Choosing to enter into spiritual community together requires a certain tenderness with each other that is kind and gentle. Many people, particularly pastors, have been treated so badly in churches and Christian organizations that we have at times wondered, Wouldn't it be something if we could at the very least be a place where people (including ourselves) encountered true kindness and gentleness over the long haul? Even if that's all we accomplished, that would be pretty big!

Brokenness: We acknowledge and honor the profound role that brokenness plays in the unfolding of the spiritual life and in the unfolding of true spiritual community. We believe that coming face to face with our weakness and sharing it together prayerfully opens us to the gift of community and also releases God's power among us, within us, beyond us (2 Corinthians 12:7-10).

Listening to Our Fear and/or Resistance. We all experience fear, particularly as we enter more deeply into community and calling. Fear causes people to behave strangely or even badly (self-protection, manipulation, combative, etc.). When it is not acknowledged, fear causes us to shrink back when perhaps God is calling us forward; however, it can also alert us to situations that are truly dangerous. Becoming a leadership community in which it is safe to articulate fear enables us to (1) exercise wisdom and ask, Is there real danger here? (2) hear God's challenge for us to be courageous, or (3) pay attention to areas where our trust is weak and needs to be strengthened.

Conflict Transformation. Someone has said that where two or three are gathered together, there will be conflict. One of the most important aspects of a community covenant is a set of concrete commitments regarding what we will do when there are significant disagreements among us or when someone begins to discern a new call from God. What is our commitment relative to discerning that together? How will we move through conflict, disagreement and strong emotion in God-honoring ways? What is the role of the group in calling individuals and the group back to these commitments during difficult times, and what is a biblical and spiritual process that we agree to adhere to? Because community at the leadership level is so challenging, this process of actually articulating covenant commitments around how we will handle conflict and embracing them together in God's presence is of utmost importance.

LEADERSHIP COMMUNITY AT ITS BEST

Articulated values are just nice-sounding words unless we enter into practical behaviors that help us live them concretely. No matter how committed we are to *being* a community and allowing our *doing* to flow out of our being, the demands of ministry always seem to want to squeeze out the time it takes to cultivate the community from which we want our leadership to emerge. We need spiritual practices that help us live our values in concrete ways; otherwise it is doubtful that we will be able to adhere to them in the rough-and-tumble of ministry.

Engaging in spiritual practices not just privately but also as a leadership community helps us live into our longing and our need for Christian community and to see kingdom work emerge with integrity from our truest identity. We want more than just another job to do; we long to see the kind of transformation in ourselves that we seek to call others to. We want more than success that is externally measured; we long for a way of life with others that is meaningful and satisfying and trustworthy. And it is this longing that keeps us faithful to our practices, drawing us back to the basics of our life together in community. When leadership flows from our commitment to being a community that gathers around the presence of Christ for ongoing transformation, our ministry is deeper and richer and more effective for ourselves and for others. Spiritual community at the leadership level is at its best when certain basic practices are in place.

When leadership community is at its best, we are finding ways to open to the presence of Christ in our midst. One of the most important ways we open to Christ's presence is to engage in rhythms of prayer at regular intervals throughout the day. In Christian tradition, this is known as "praying the hours" or "the daily office." These prayers lead us to turn our hearts toward God in ways that are appropriate for whatever part of the day we are in. When we are working together we begin the morning with praise, affirming God's love for us and committing the work of the day to him. At midday, when tasks are pressing in and human effort is at its height, we stop to renew our awareness of God's presence, to rest in him and to ask for his peace and guidance. In the evening we place the cares of the day in God's hand and make intercession for ourselves and others. If we are together on retreat, we close the day with night prayer, confessing our sins, celebrating God's presence with us during the day and asking him to be with us as we rest.

During these times, Scripture is read without comment, giving God the opportunity to address us directly through his Word. The Gospel readings in particular help us stay connected to the person of Christ as the model for our life and work. In this way, the Spirit of Christ has access to us throughout the day, giving us perspective, assurance or guidance as we need it beyond human orchestration.

When leadership community is at its best, we are attending to our relationships. We are taking time to listen to each other, care for each other with a word or a touch, and pray for each other whether we are together or apart. As we work together, we seek to find ways to be loving toward each other, to affirm one another's gifts and unique contributions to our shared work. When there is misunderstanding or hurt in a particular relationship or if there is hesitancy or resistance to a particular direction we are taking, we do our best to create time and space to pay attention, believing that the most important thing we can do is love each other well. One of the greatest accomplishments of Jesus' time here on earth was that "he loved his own . . . to the end" (John 13:1). Loving each other well takes time and attention. But if we fail at that, we have failed at the one thing Jesus wants most from us and for us.

When leadership community is at its best, we are resting and retreating. Building time for a leadership community to go on retreat can be challenging but it is also one of the most significant aspects of our life together. Retreats are not merely off-site planning meetings so that we can work longer than we would if we were back at the office. They are not conference-type events full of programming, noisy activity and too much information. A spiritual retreat is a time apart when we move more slowly, take time to rest, have extended time for solitude and silent listening, share our journeys and key learnings, eat together and enjoy one another's company. The ideal for us has been two or three leadership retreats a year; this is a lot for busy people, and we have not always been able to accomplish this. But we have found that when we compromise these times, we become tired and disconnected from ourselves, each other and God himself, and then we are back to having compromised some of our deepest values.

When leadership community is at its best, we are living within our limits. There is something deeply spiritual about honoring the limitations of our lives and the boundaries of what God has given us to do as leaders. Narcissistic leaders are always looking beyond their sphere of influence with visions of grandiosity far out of proportion to what is actually being given. Living within our limits means living within the finiteness of who we are as individuals and as a community—the limits of time and space, the limits of our physical, emotional, relational and spiritual capacities, the limits of our stage of life as an organization and the individuals who make up the organization, and the limits of the calling that God has given. It means doing this and not that. It means doing this much and not more.

When we refuse to live within our limits (one of my deepest temptations), we wear out ourselves and those who lead with us. We compromise the quality of our relationships with God and the people around us. We compromise our effectiveness at doing the things we have been called to do. To live within our limits is to live humbly as the creature and not the Creator. Only God is infinite; the rest of us need to be very clear about what we are to be about in any given moment and say no to everything else.

When leadership community is at its best, we are moving forward in our work on the basis of discernment. One of the defining characteristics of any spiritual community is a shared desire and willingness to act on the basis of discernment rather than human planning and strategic maneuvering. We are not opposed to planning; in fact, that is an important second step. But we understand that discernment— listening deeply for God's direction—must precede any planning we do. Even though we are accustomed to the strategic planning process and are in some cases quite drawn to it, the truth is that every time we have made decisions purely from strategic thinking without providing some space for discernment, we have gotten out ahead of ourselves and made mistakes. We have experienced this most clearly in our scheduling. When we look at things strategically, it always makes sense to schedule more events, but this usually means we end up with more than we can handle. However, when we listen to what God is saying to us in the deeper places of our being, we usually find that less is more and we can plan accordingly. These are humbling lessons to learn, but they can shape our future planning if we learn these lessons well.

When there has been a place for discernment in our decision-making process, we are able to move confidently and with a sure step toward our deepest calling rather than falling prey to the frenetic pace that often develops when we just think our way into things. Knowing how to discern God's will together is such a key aspect of the soul of leadership that the next chapter is devoted to it.

No Guarantees

Even when good attention is being paid to our life in community, there are times when relationships between Christian leaders fall apart, and we are naive not to be prepared for it. Relational breakdown and betrayal happened to Moses (the incident with Korah comes to mind), it happened with Paul and Barnabas (regarding John Mark), and it happened with Jesus (Judas's betrayal). These are very painful times in the life of any leader. During such times, the thing that is most helpful is to stay close to Jesus—as overly simple as that sounds. What I mean by "staying close to Jesus" is to enter the story of Jesus' life and allow his story to guide our response.

During a season when I was experiencing some relational heartache, the discipline of following the lectionary took me into the life of Christ in a way that caught me completely off-guard. On a random day in May, I found myself in the story of Judas's betrayal—which was not a story I would have chosen at the time. For one thing, I would not have been presumptuous enough to equate my own situation with Judas's betrayal. And for another, when you are going through your own relational difficulties, the story of Judas and Jesus is not all that comforting! It was not Holy Week (which is when I would have expected to be reading it) and it wasn't a Gospel reading (which is where I was most accustomed to finding it); it was a reading from Acts 1 in the aftermath of the crucifixion and resurrection. The surprise of finding myself in this point of Scripture so unexpectedly let me know that I needed to sit up and pay attention. As I read this story in the midst of my own hurt and pain, it turned out to be exactly what I needed.

In this passage Peter is the one speaking, trying to help the shaky little group of Christ-followers who were left after Jesus' death and resurrection make sense of all they had been through. Part of the experience they needed to make sense of was Judas's betrayal. Their questions were the same as mine would have been: What was *that* all about? How did we all trust someone who was so untrustworthy? Why had Jesus let this person hang around so long, knowing that he was so dangerous? Could one of us be capable of the same kind of betrayal?

To those who remained together praying and waiting on God for what was next, Peter spoke very honestly. He acknowledged that Judas had been an important part of the community and had been allotted a share in the ministry. He gave the facts about what had happened, and then he offered a perspective based on his understanding of Scripture. He even went so far as to say that this betrayal had to happen in order to fulfill what had been foretold by David. He did not sugarcoat the situation. He did not spin it. But he did help the community find meaning in it. This in itself was very healing, as surely there was great grief in the room as he was speaking. Maybe there was even quiet weeping.

Then Peter led them gently into the next step of the healing process, which was to discern who should take Judas's place. "Lord, you know everyone's heart. Show us which one of these two you have chosen to take the place in this ministry and apostleship from which Judas turned aside to go to his own place" (Acts 1:24-25). What a gentle and yet wise and truthful prayer to pray at such a tender time in this community's life.

One of the hard things that Judas's story teaches us is that we cannot control others and their choices. Judas had been given the ministry and apostleship as much as any of the others, but his choice to "turn aside and go to his own place" was his to make. I wonder if Jesus let Judas stay around as long he did—even knowing what he knew—because up to the very end he was hoping that Judas would make a different choice. But he didn't. And when this happens, all we can do is let the other go. Our free will is something that Jesus honors with us, and it is something that we must honor with others.

This kind of acceptance of what *is* has been such a hard lesson for me to learn that I'm sure it is why God has had to teach it to me in many ways! I have had to learn that someone else's personal choice does not necessarily mean that I have failed as a leader or that the community has failed. Being able to distinguish between our own issues (for which we must take responsibility) and others' issues (which are not our responsibility) is something we have to work through very carefully with God in personal self-examination and in trustworthy community. No matter what we determine, the loss does pull the community into a period of transition and decision-making—just as it did for this little band of Christ-followers. Peter's clarity, his honesty, the inner authority that came from his own (recent) purgation process held them together and helped those who were left to keep going.

If we stay close to Jesus, we might also notice that between the time of Judas's betrayal and the crucifixion—presumably two of the hardest experiences of Jesus' ministry life—he prayed for unity among his followers. Even though he had already been betrayed and would be once again, he still believed in the possibility of unity among his followers. His heartfelt cry to his Father so close to the time of his death was "Protect them . . . so that they may be one" (John 17:11). It wasn't "protect them so that they can preach the gospel or build the kingdom or defeat Satan"—worthy as all those things would have been. It was *protect them so that they may be one.* Maybe that is because our oneness in Christ *is*

> *Therefore, let him who until now has had the privilege of living a*
> *common Christian life with other Christians praise God's grace*
> *from the bottom of his heart. Let him thank God on his knees and*
> *declare: It is grace, nothing but grace, that we are allowed to live*
> *in community with Christian brethren.*
>
> DIETRICH BONHOEFFER, *LIFE TOGETHER*

the kingdom, it *is* preaching the gospel, it *is* how we defeat Satan.

For Christian people, unity is not just one good priority among many. It seemed to be all Jesus wanted as everything else fell away and he faced his death. For those of us who are leaders in Christ's kingdom, there is nothing more important than seeking this unity with all our hearts. Even when we fall short of achieving it, we believe that all things have already been reconciled through Christ and we do whatever is ours to do to be at peace with all people.

BEYOND ISOLATION

Early in our life together, our leadership community had the privilege of retreating at a Benedictine monastery and listening to one of the brothers who had been a priest in this religious community for fifty years talk about his life as a monk. Specifically, we asked what had enabled these brothers to stay together in community for so long and how we might do the same. One of the first things he talked about was their commitment to stability. With penetrating eyes and surety of speech, he told us in no uncertain terms to "pick a community and stay with it; pick a path and stay on it."

I have never forgotten his statement, because it is so different from the way my own life in leadership has been shaped. We Protestant Christians do not have a context for this kind of commitment to stability. We shop for community the way we shop for a new house or a new car, and "picking a community and staying with it" goes completely against our consumer mindset. For those of us in pastoral ministry, the church is our job, and we would be hard pressed to experience it as a community to which we are committed for the long haul. Depending on the polity of our church or denomination, it may not even be our choice to make. But Moses' story and the example of other religious communities calls us to at least consider moving beyond our culturally conditioned patterns of isolation, transience and independence to the richness and interdependence of a leadership community that is strong enough and stable enough to provide *ongoing* spiritual guidance for those whom we are leading.

How interesting that when we open up our loneliness in God's presence, we are led eventually to a commitment to certain persons, certain values, a certain journey, and then we are called to remain faithful to those commitments. To cure the loneliness of isolation,

> we need to find a still point inside a community of faith. We need to find a home. . . . Finding a home is not, in the end, so much a question of finding a building, a city, a country or a place where we feel we belong. More deeply, finding a home is a question of finding another heart or a community of hearts wherein we feel at one, safe, warm, comfortable, able to be ourselves, secure enough to express both faith and affection. . . . There is an answer to that loneliness, a new home inside that community of faith.

PRACTICE

Take some time in quiet to breathe deeply and let yourself feel the burdens you are carrying and how weighty they have become. If the loneliness that Moses expressed in Numbers 11 is something you are experiencing, let yourself sit with your loneliness and then say what you need to say to God about it. If you feel that you are on the brink of disaster as

Moses was, tell God about that too. If it fits, use the following prayer to
help you say what you need to say to God just now and to allow him to
give you a glimpse of what or who might be possible for you.

■   ■   ■

Hear me quickly, Lord
for my mind soon wanders to other things
   I am more familiar with
     and more concerned about
       than I am with you.

Words will not do, Lord.
Listen to my tears,
  for I have lost much
   and fear more.
Listen to my sweat,
  for I wake at night,
    overwhelmed by darkness and strange dreams.
Listen to my sighs,
  for my longing surges like the sea—
  urgent, mysterious, beckoning.
Listen to my growling gut,
  for I hunger for bread and intimacy.
Listen to my curses,
  for I am angry at the way the world
  comes down on me sometimes
   and I sometimes on it.
Listen to my crackling knuckles,
  for I hold very tightly to myself
   and anxiously squeeze myself

into others' expectations
and them into mine,
and then shake my fists at you
for disappointing me.

Listen to my footfalls,
for I stumble to bring good tidings to someone.
Listen to my groans,
for I ache towards healing.
Listen to my worried weariness,
for my work matters much to me
and needs help.
Listen to my tension,
for I ache toward accepting who I am
and who I cannot be.
Listen to my hunched back,
For sometimes I can't bear
the needs and demands of the world anymore
and want to put it down,
give it back to you.

Listen to my laughter,
for there are friends
and mercy
and something urges me to thank.
Listen to my humming,
for sometimes I catch all unaware
the rhythms of creation
and then music without words
rises in me to meet it,
and there is the joy of romping children
and dancing angels.

Listen to my blinking eyes,
   for at certain moments
      when sunlight strikes just right,
      or stars pierce the darkness just enough,
      or clouds roll around just so,
      or snow kisses the world into quietness,
   everything is suddenly transparent . . .
and something in me is pure enough
   for an instant
to see your kingdom in a glance,
and so to praise you in a gasp—
   quick,
      then gone,
         but it is enough.

Listen to me quickly, Lord.

TED LODER, *GUERRILLAS OF GRACE*

12

FINDING
GOD'S WILL
TOGETHER

Whenever the cloud lifted from over the tent,

then the Israelites would set out; and in the place where

the cloud settled down, there the Israelites would camp.

At the command of the LORD the Israelites would set out,

and at the command of the LORD they would camp.

NUMBERS 9:17-18

It was a conversation similar to many I have had with Christian leaders. A pastor from a large church was telling me that his church was going through a major transition as its leaders tried to respond to the growth they were experiencing. They had outgrown their facility (a good problem to have!), so the obvious question was, "Will we add onto our facility or will we start another church?"

But clearly this was only the tip of the iceberg. Beneath the surface larger questions lurked: What should be our emphasis now? Does our mission still capture what we feel called to? Is the leadership structure effective for what is emerging now? Can we keep going this way or will we burn ourselves out if we add a building campaign and more people and activities to our plates?

Sensing the weight that he was carrying, I probed a little deeper and asked, "How are you going about answering these questions? Does your leadership team have a process for discerning God's will in these matters?"

A look of disorienting awareness crossed his face as he realized that the answer to the question was no. After recovering a bit, he said, "But we always have a time of prayer at the beginning of our meetings."

THE HEART OF SPIRITUAL LEADERSHIP

Many of us have a vague idea that there should be something different about our leadership as Christians—particularly if we are leading a church or organization with a spiritual purpose—but that difference usually gets reduced to a perfunctory prayer at the beginning of a meeting, and sometimes even that gets lost in the shuffle! What is it, then, that distinguishes spiritual leadership from other kinds of leadership? What distinguishes a spiritual journey from other journeys that one might embark upon?

At the heart of *spiritual* leadership and *spiritual* journeying is discernment—the capacity to recognize and respond to the presence and the activity of God both personally and in community. The Israelite journey is really a story of ongoing discernment. It is a story of a group of human beings who learned how to recognize the presence of God and then followed that Presence wherever it went. For Moses as their leader, this involved entering into God's presence regularly and routinely, asking God what he should do and then leading the people in that way. Moses' ability to trust God and to listen and respond obediently to his instructions was so crucial to the Israelites' survival that the one time he failed to follow God's instruction fully (when he struck the rock to provide water for the people rather than speaking to it as God had commanded) there were grave consequences (Numbers 20:10-13).

For the community as a whole, the journey involved ongoing response to the presence of God as they experienced it in the pillar of cloud by day and the pillar of fire by night. When the presence of God moved, they followed it, and when the presence of God stayed, they stayed (Numbers 9). It was as simple as that. It is no wonder that when Moses recapped the Israelite journey, he emphasized how important discernment had been to the whole operation. He reminded the people of the time God told them to choose leaders to serve as judges under Moses and that the heart of their spiritual leadership was the ability to be "wise" and "discerning" (Deuteronomy 1:13).

Later on he spoke about wisdom and discernment as defining characteristics for the nation of Israel, characteristics that would be recognized and revered by other nations. He pointed out that discernment is about intimacy with God—an intimacy that other nations did not have with their gods and would marvel at. "You . . . will show your wisdom and discernment to the peoples, who . . . will say, 'Surely this great nation is a wise and discerning people!' For what other great nation has a god so near to it as the LORD our God is whenever we call to him?" (Deuteronomy 4:6-7). This amazing opportunity to be intimate with God and discern his ways was at the heart of their identity, and it was one of the main things that would distinguish them from other nations.

A CULTURE OF DISCERNMENT

In our day, discernment is much easier said than done. We do not have a pillar of cloud to follow by day and a pillar of fire to follow by night. We do not get to talk with God face to face or listen to his voice thundering on the top of Mount Horeb. Instead, we must rely on the more subtle dynamics of the Holy Spirit witnessing with the human spirit about things that are true (Romans 8:16). Discernment presents unique challenges in contemporary Western culture, because it requires us to move beyond our reliance on cognition and intellectual hard work to a place of deep listening and response to the Spirit of God within us and among us. It is one thing to rely on what sometimes feels like a subjective approach when it pertains to one's personal life; it feels much riskier when our decisions involve large budgets, other people's financial investments, the lives of multiple staff, reports to high-powered boards, and serving a congregation or customer base with their expectations. Is there a trustworthy process for actively seeking God relative to decisions we are making?

The *spiritual* leader is distinguished by his or her commitment and ability to guide the discernment process so the community can affirm a shared sense of God's desire for them and move forward on that basis. The practice of leadership discernment, like any other Christian discipline, is a means of creating space for God's activity in our lives. It is one way we can make ourselves available so that he can do for us what we cannot do for ourselves. Through the practice of discernment in community we open ourselves to the wisdom of God that is beyond human wisdom but is available to us when we ask for it.

Discernment does not take place in a vacuum, nor does it take place by accident. Spiritual community is the context for discernment, so an important prerequisite for leadership in discernment is to establish the leadership group as a community for discernment. This means that our life together as leaders is grounded in prayer and other spiritual practices. It means we maintain our commitment to Scripture, silence, listening (to God and each other), worship and intercession, self-examination and confession *as the container* for the discernment process, no matter how much we are tempted to let them slip on any given day.

Romans 12:2 indicates that the ability to discern the will of God is a natural byproduct of spiritual transformation in community. Paul says, "Do not be conformed to this world, but be transformed by the renewing of your minds, *so that* you may discern what is the will of God—what is good and acceptable and perfect." This passage establishes a *causal* (not casual) relationship between the journey of spiritual transformation and the ability to discern God's will both personally and in community. Our ability to discern what we should *do* flows from our commitment to *be* together in life-transforming ways. Conversely, when our commitment to spiritual practices in community slips, we become muddled in our capacity to be truly discerning. Rather than acting from a clear sense of God's desire for us, we can be driven by our own agendas. Rather than experiencing God's peace, we might become frantic. Rather than finding clarity, it is easy to become lost in a swirl of inner and outer chaos.

DYNAMICS OF DISCERNMENT

The impulse to discern—to know and do the will of God—is a spiritual dynamic that goes against human willfulness. When individuals, leadership groups or congregations have a desire to become more discerning, this in itself is evidence of God at work. While it is natural for a Christian person to want to do the will of God, it cannot be assumed that this desire is always at the forefront of leaders' awareness when they come together to make decisions. When this desire is at all in evidence or people start to articulate their longing for it, we should thank God for it, fan it into flame, guide the group in articulating a commitment to it and be wise in setting forth a concrete process for entering in.

As we cultivate spiritual community, the desire and the capacity for discernment begin to develop naturally, and we become more practiced at recognizing and responding to the Spirit of God within us and among us. This is a mark of Christian maturity. By its very nature Christian discernment is a spiritual practice because it is about Spirit—the Spirit of God who is the third person of the Trinity and can be listened to and responded to. Discernment is always a gift given by the Spirit to spiritual people. "Those who are unspiritual do not receive the gifts of God's Spirit, for they are foolishness to them, and they are unable to understand them because they are spiritually discerned" (1 Corinthians 2:14).

Discernment is a way of seeing that is first of all a habit, enabling us to see the works of God as they are being revealed in our lives. It is a way of being in which we are steeped in listening and responding to the Spirit.

As important as the practices of discernment are, it would be improper to list them before the habit of discernment, because if the Holy Spirit has not been welcomed into the life of the discerner, practices of discernment will be empty and impotent. The habit of discernment constitutes a way of being, by which we are steeped in spirituality as a way of life; and spirituality becomes as necessary as the air we breathe. The habit of spirituality precedes the practices of discernment.

The habit of discernment is important preparation for those times when we need to make decisions and we are called to intentionally and actively seek God's will. During such times the spiritual leader calls people into the *practice* of discernment. Discernment is grounded in our belief that God is good, that his intentions toward us are always good and that he has the power to carry them out. Without this fundamental conviction it would be hard, if not impossible, to give ourselves freely and fully to the discernment process. It is hard to open ourselves fully to Someone we don't trust to be good to us in the deepest ways.

Discernment is also grounded in the belief that the call to love God and to love others is our ultimate calling as Christian people—whether in the day-to-day choices of our lives or in the larger decisions facing a govern-

> *God's will is the best thing that could*
>
> *happen to us under any circumstances.*
>
> DANNY MORRIS AND CHARLES OLSEN,
> *DISCERNING GOD'S WILL TOGETHER*

ing body. Thus in every decision we make we could hope that somewhere along the way someone will ask, "What does love call us to?"

EXPLORING A PROCESS FOR LEADERSHIP DISCERNMENT

Community discernment at the leadership level is not mechanical, nor is it always linear. As we become more comfortable with the process, we experience it less as a step-by-step procedure and more as a creative mix of the following dynamic elements. Although the first several moves need to take place in order (for reasons that will become obvious) as a group practices together over time, different elements of discernment will happen quite naturally in ways and at times that are unique to you.

Preparing for community discernment. The first step toward entering into a discernment process is to *clarify the question for discernment.* Not all questions warrant a full discernment process. Some questions, such as choosing a computer system, might be answered with a fifteen-minute, fact-based discussion. However, there are other questions that require a different level of attention and prayerfulness from the entire leadership group, particularly those that shape our identity, our policies, our values and our direction. The hiring of key personnel, those who will wield significant influence, should also be a matter for discernment.

Even when we think we know what the question is, there may be a larger question lurking underneath the rest, a question that holds even greater significance for us. The question about a new building project might deepen into a question about mission and values and whether a new building might or might not help us stay true to these. What starts out as a meeting to set strategy gives way to the deeper question of whether we are pushing our own agenda or whether God is really opening up new opportunities. What begins as a question about event scheduling raises a more far-reaching concern about pace of life and whether we are working and living together in such a way that we honor true human limitations and create space in our lives for loving God and others. Thus discernment begins with clarifying the question and perhaps even listening for the deeper question.

It is also important that we *involve the right people*. A prerequisite for community discernment is that the individuals involved are committed to the process of personal transformation. It is essential that these individuals are experienced in personal discernment as both habit and practice in their own decision-making. One very common leadership mistake is to think that we can take a group of undiscerning individuals and expect them to show up in a leadership setting and all of a sudden become discerning! Many boards and elder groups are composed primarily of people who have been successful in business ventures but may not have had much preparation or experience in the area of spiritual discernment. If this is the case, we might need to slowly change the makeup of the leadership group, or we might need to provide teaching and training before embarking on a discernment process. (Note: for a substantive treatment of the habit and practice of personal discernment, please refer to chapter 6 of my book *Sacred Rhythms*.)

Another aspect of involving the right people is to think outside the box about who else needs to be involved in the process. We can become so stuck in organizational silos that we overlook others who might have important contributions to make to the discernment process. In addition to those who are already a part of the board, the staff or the management team, we might consider: Who else has gifts of wisdom and discernment that we value? Who has information and experience that might help us? Who are the influencers that might be able to help communicate the outcomes of our process in an inviting way to the larger community when the time comes?

There can even be several levels of involvement. There is the discernment group—those who are responsible in the end to vote or in some other way make the decision about how to move forward. These should be fully engaged in the entire process. There are also voices of input that the group needs to hear in order to make a fully informed decision—those who will be affected by the decision, those who have pertinent experiences, those who have expertise or have done research in the area being considered, those who actually have to carry out the course of action that we decide on (key staff or volunteers, administrative or operations personnel, and the like). These folks don't need to be present for everything, nor do they need to have a vote, but we will probably make wiser and more realistic decisions if we are open to their expertise.

One other type of person we might consider involving is someone who has practice and training in the art and practice of discernment. This could be a spiritual director, a *discernmentarian* (someone who guides the discernment process, much as a parliamentarian guides the process of majority rule), a clerk or convener (as such a role is defined in Quaker circles), or a sage. While each of these terms has different nuances, they all apply to someone who does not have a vested interest in any particular outcome and is able to listen prayerfully, call for silence as needed, perhaps guide the process, or comment at different points regarding what they are hearing and how they think the Spirit might be moving the group.

We also need to *establish guiding values and principles* for the discernment process. Discernment with others at the leadership level requires an extraordinary amount of safety in each other's presence, along with great clarity about what values govern the process. There are certain values that we might want to consider agreeing together not to violate for any reason, no matter how expedient it might seem. One of these values would be our commitment to trustworthy relationships in community.

Somewhere along the line, we need to grapple with the fact that learning to come together in unity is our first and most enduring task as we pattern our relationships after Christ's commitment to his own disciples. We cannot just assume these values; we must talk about them and seek to live into them with great vigor and intent. It might even be helpful to establish a written covenant with each other regarding the values and practices that will govern our deliberations.

Even if a community covenant is already in place, it is good at the beginning of a discernment process—especially if there is disagreement or lots of vested interest—to go over the covenant again and reaffirm that the group gathered for discernment will be committed to each other and to the integrity of the relationships above all else. There needs to be some basic agreement that to compromise core values for any reason would mean that we have compromised our essence and then we would not have much of value to offer others.

In a community that gathers for discernment, leaders are committed to moving beyond the kind of maneuvering and posturing that often takes place in leadership settings and are willing to tell the truth to the best of their ability. As Christians we believe God works through *all* truth—even truth that seems as if it might slow us down or complicate matters or take us into uncharted territory—to bring forth the gift of discernment. Even when the truth is hard, we take great pains to affirm the courage that it takes for each one of us to bring God-given truth to the discernment process. We will be committed to honoring one another's deep reservations or resistance to a particular direction or decision, trusting the Spirit of God in that person, and will wait for deeper understanding and unity. I have never seen a leadership group regret the decision to honor each other in this way. In fact, in leadership groups I have been a part of, God has often used this principle to save us from ourselves!

As we do the hard work of preparing, it is good to remind ourselves of how painstaking and even tedious God was in providing guidance for the Israelites' life in community. In my own Bible reading I have often skipped from the Ten Commandments to the next exciting story because I did not have the patience to wade through the detail and tedium of Leviticus. But now I get it. The whole journey would have been lost without those guidelines! The group would have fallen apart in the wilderness, and they wouldn't have survived without each other. Without such specific guidelines, practices and disciplines to hold them under God's (and Moses') guidance, the stresses and pressures would have been too much for them. There would not have been a group to enter into the Promised Land.

Entering into the discernment process. A true discernment process begins with a commitment to *pray without ceasing.* This requires much more than a perfunctory prayer at the beginning of a meeting. In fact, it involves several kinds of praying throughout the entire process. When the question for discernment has been clarified, the community for discernment is assembled and guiding principles have been established, we can begin with a prayer of quiet trust like the one found in Psalm 131, in which the psalmist acknowledges his utter dependence upon God in the face of matters "too great and too marvelous for me" (v. 1). A different kind of spirit descends upon us when we enter into decision-making from this stance. When we sense that the process is getting out of hand, that human dynamics are distracting us from real issues, that we are stuck, that we are applying nothing more than human effort to the decision we face, it can be very helpful for the leader to call the group back to this prayer of quiet trust, along with some time for silence. This gives us the opportunity to shift back into a position of trust rather than being completely reliant on our own human striving.

We need to also pray for *indifference.* This is not the kind of indifference that we associate with apathy; rather, it is the prayer that we would be indifferent to everything but the will of God. Indifference in the discernment process means that I am indifferent to matters of ego, prestige, organizational politics, personal advantage, personal comfort or favor, or even my own pet project. As Danny Morris and Charles Olsen put it: "God's will, nothing more, nothing less, nothing else."

The prayer for indifference can be a very challenging prayer for us to pray, because most times we enter into decision-making with strong opinions and more than a little self-interest. It takes time, and often a death to self is required before we can see God's will taking shape in our lives. Here we ask ourselves the question, *What needs to die in me in order for the will of God to come forth in and among us?* As a part of the discernment process, each person needs to do their own spiritual work around this question, and the group needs to be honest about it. Depending on the level of trust in the group, it might even be a good idea to ask, "How many are indifferent?" and then let each person talk about where they are with that question. Some might be able to report that by God's grace they have come to the point of indifference. Others might say that they are attached to one outcome or another for whatever reason but are still praying about it and asking God to bring them to a place of being indifferent to anything but the will of God.

Mary, the mother of Jesus, is a model of what it means to be indifferent. Her prayer "Here am I, the servant of the Lord; let it be with me according to your word" (Luke 1:38) is a wonderful expression of the kind of indifference we are talking about here. Her story can be helpful to us when we are struggling to let go and come to a place of indifference in our own discernment process.

As challenging as this part of the process may be, it is time and energy well spent. If we do not reach the point of indifference or if we are not at least honest about the fact that we are not indifferent, the discernment process becomes little more than a rigged election! Even the process of sharing where we are with others can help us loosen our grip on our own agenda and open ourselves to the wisdom of the group.

When we have reached a point of indifference, we are finally ready to *pray for wisdom,* which God promises to bestow on us generously when we ask (James 1:5). Indifference is an important prerequisite to the prayer for wisdom, because the wisdom of God is often the foolishness of this world; indifference to matters of our own ego, in particular, prepares us to receive this gift.

A true discernment process continues with *listening on many levels*. This is the heart of the process and perhaps the part that takes the longest. First of all we must listen deeply to the experience(s) that caused us to be asking this question in the first place. When the New Testament believers were faced with the question of whether Gentiles should be required to be circumcised in order to be saved (Acts 15), they entered into a time of deep listening: to the conversion experience of the Gentiles, to the perspectives of the people who were with them, to the questions and debate of the Pharisees, to Peter's sense of personal calling to the Gentiles, to Paul and Barnabas's accounts of signs and wonders, to James's exposition of Scripture connecting this experience to the words of the prophets in the Old Testament as he located their story in the larger Story of God's redemptive purposes.

Finally, out of all that listening James dared to state what he felt God was saying in it all: that the church would not impose any further burden on Gentile converts beyond the essentials of the faith. The listening process had been so thorough that when James summarized it succinctly, it was clear to everyone that the wisdom of God had been given (Acts 15:13-21). In a way he functioned as a spiritual director who sat back and listened and then named what he heard God saying in the group.

This story illustrates that the discernment process involves a major commitment to listening with love and attention to our experiences, to the inner promptings of the Holy Spirit deep within ourselves and others, to Scripture and Christian tradition, to pertinent facts and information, to those who will be affected most deeply by our decisions, to that place in us where God's Spirit witnesses with our spirit about those things that are true. We need to pay particular attention to distress, confusion and desolation. Even the more difficult emotions need to be honored.

It is also good to notice whether or not the discernment process is being dominated by the opinions of those with stronger personalities or those who talk the most. One way to make sure that all the voices that need to be heard are being heard is for the chairperson or the convener to ask, after several people have spoken more than once, "Is there anyone who hasn't spoken yet who would like to say something that hasn't been said?" Sometimes the most important thing we need to hear or the perspective that shifts the meeting or gets us unstuck is offered by the person who is the quietest and needs the most encouragement to speak.

Another part of the listening process is willingness to enter back into silence and "listen within" when human dynamics are getting out of control, when there have been too many words, when the words are no longer helping or when the process gets stuck. Discernment requires self- and other-awareness, and silence creates space for that. In silence we can become aware of our emotions, thoughts, experiences, sins, temptations, indifference (or lack thereof) so that we can see how these are affecting our participation and can take responsibility for ourselves. With a little bit of distance, we may also be able to observe dynamics in the group and name them in a way that is helpful and opens up the possibility of shifting it somehow. Most of all, we can come back to an awareness of others and the gift that they are—in our similarity and our diversity. In the silence we can come back to a place of honoring each other and the complexity of the situation.

Silence can help us cease striving and rest in God, it can bring calm to the chaos we might be feeling, it can give space for us to deal with our own inner dynamics, and it can help us listen to God—which is often what is most needed at such times. The words that follow such silence are often characterized by deeper wisdom and truer insight than what was said prior to it.

Completing the discernment process. After all the listening has taken place, it is time to *select an option that seems consistent with what God is doing among you.* Discernment does not always come with as much clarity as it did for the New Testament elders in Acts 15. When it's not clear, you might select an option or two, seek to improve upon those options so that they are the best they can possibly be, and then weigh them to see which one seems most consistent with what God is doing among you. The Quakers, who are known for their discernment practices, would encourage folks to "place each path near the heart" and see which one brings consolation or desolation. On which option does the Spirit of God seem to rest? What is the fruit of each option? Several other questions that can be helpful in weighing the alternatives: Is there a Scripture that God brings to mind that is pertinent to the issue we are facing? What is the thing that God is making natural and easy? What brings a sense of lightness and peace even in the midst of challenge? Is there an option that enables us to do something before we do everything?

Discernment at this level takes a great deal of maturity, because when we talk about matters of consolation and desolation, we are talking about more than surface emotion. We are talking about the ability to pay attention to the subtle inner dynamics that move us toward God and toward greater abandonment to his will and those that move us away from God and the life of faith. To put it bluntly,

> this way of discerning depends greatly on our spiritual and psychological maturity. If we are ambivalent and divided by chaotic emotions and neurotic conditions, our affective states will provide no positive guidance. Our task will be to understand our condition and bring order and discipline into our affective life. But as we come to achieve that discipline, in proportion as "we die and our lives are lives hidden with Christ in God," discernment becomes more effective.

Once the group has narrowed it down to one or two options, it is important to give time for individuals to *seek inner confirmation*. Sometimes in the emotion of a meeting we can get carried away by what is happening in the moment. People need some time apart from the group to become quiet in God's presence, to pray and think through the options, and to notice whether they are at peace with the decisions being made. It is good to take a break (a few minutes, an hour, a day or even a week) and then come back together and check in with each other to see what God has been saying in our quiet listening. If people are experiencing deep inner peace with one of the options, then affirm that together. If anyone is still having reservations or experiencing questions or resistance, honor them by listening to what they are experiencing and see what God has to say to you in it. Perhaps one element of a particular option needs to be tweaked, or perhaps a larger adjustment needs to be made. Trust God to work through this person's hesitation to make the option that we are choosing the best and the wisest it can be.

Agree together. Once the leadership group has thoroughly explored the different options and dealt with questions and resistances that the group has raised, hopefully clarity emerges pointing toward one of the options or some combination of them as particularly graced by God with wisdom and truth. In the Quaker Friends tradition, what is more important than the decision itself is the quality of life together and a sense that they have found the decision that is best for the group. In an unpublished source a Quaker pastor put it like this: "Unity is the fundamental marker that God's direction has been discerned."

When the gift of discernment has been given, those responsible for providing leadership can look at each other and say, "To the best of our ability, we agree that this particular path is God's will for us, so this is the direction we will go." Then we rest in God, thanking him for his presence with us and for the gift of discernment as it has been given. Then we are ready, as the old Nike commercial admonishes, to "Just do it!"

But discernment is not the endgame. The endgame is to actually *do* the will of God as we have come to understand it. Now is the time to bring in the strategic planners and the consultants, if you need them. Now it is time to move forward with confidence that "the one who calls you is faithful and he will do this" (1 Thessalonians 5:24 NIV).

With all this book's emphasis on the soul of leadership, you may have been wondering how you get somewhere! Well, you get somewhere by discerning God's will and doing it together. That is what spiritual community and spiritual leadership are all about.

PRACTICE

Allow your solitude today to be a time to reflect honestly about discernment as the heart of your spiritual leadership. Is discernment a way of life for you and for those who are leading with you? Is there an area of decision-making where discernment is needed, where you know that no amount of human thinking and strategizing will provide you with the wisdom you need? Take a few minutes to rest in God's presence and experience your longing for God's direction relative to this matter. Notice whether you are indifferent to anything but the will of God or whether you are attached to a particular outcome. Allow yourself to envision what it might be like for your leadership group to become a community for discernment and live more fully into this spiritual practice. If you believe the group isn't ready to embark on the whole process, is there one piece of it that you could introduce as a way of beginning?

The following prayer is one our leadership community has prayed together over and over again as we have faced issues both great and small in which we have desperately needed God's guidance. Pray it alone and pray it with those who lead with you as you face decisions together. Let it become a prayer that carries your leadership community across the threshold from decision-making to discernment.

■　■　■

Oh God, by whom we are guided in judgment,
and who raises up for us light in the darkness:
Grant us, in all our doubts and uncertainties,
the grace to ask what you would have us to do;
that your spirit of wisdom may save us from all false choices,
and in your straight path we may not stumble;
through Jesus Christ our Lord.
Amen.

BOOK OF COMMON PRAYER

13

Reenvisioning the Promised Land

The LORD said to him, "This is the land of which

I swore to Abraham, to Isaac, and to Jacob. . . . I have

let you see it with your eyes, but you shall not cross

over there." Then Moses, the servant of the LORD,

died there in the land of Moab,

at the LORD's command.

Deuteronomy 34:4-5

Strengthening the soul of our leadership is an invitation that begins, continues and ends with seeking God in the crucible of ministry. It is an invitation to stay connected with our own soul—that very private place where God's Spirit and my spirit dwell together in union—and to lead from that place. The choice to lead from our soul is a vulnerable approach to leadership, because the soul is more tender than the mind or the ego. This is a place where we don't have all the answers—or at least not necessarily when everybody wants them! It is a place where we are not in control; God is. It is a place where the quickest way is not always the best way, because the transformation that is happening in us is more important than getting where we think we need to go.

As we stay faithful to the journey into the center of our being where God dwells, we are freed from our bondage to the expectations of others and our own inner compulsions, we are less and less mesmerized by human voices, less and less manipulated by the expectations of others and more and more given over to God. In our encounters with God we die not only to the expectations of others but also to ourselves—our addiction to performing, to looking good and being perfect, to attaining more status than is good for us.

Because we are experiencing ourselves to be deeply loved by God, we begin to recognize an inner freedom that is beyond what we ever thought possible. We can handle an enormous amount of success and failure without losing our identity. We can loosen our grip on the things we have been attached to—money, success, some way we had come to see ourselves or our relationships or our ministry—and receive them as gifts without being overly identified with them because they do not define us anymore. We find that we are able to love others deeply and unconditionally because we have faced ourselves—the darkness and the light—and we have found ourselves to be unconditionally loved by God. We are able to love and lead with abandonment and freedom because we have nothing ultimately to lose.

All of this is radically counter to the current cultural milieu, but we find that if we are willing to lead from this place, we finally have something real to offer that actually corresponds to what people around us are seeking. And, the *quality* of our leadership is decidedly different.

Rather than leading from the unconscious patterns of the false self, I am leading from a self that is being transformed by my encounters with God in solitude and silence.

Rather than leading from frenetic busyness, I am leading at a measured pace, taking time to notice the burning bushes in my life.

Rather than leading from a place of overstimulation and exhaustion, I am discovering rhythms of work and rest, silence and word, stillness and action that God built into the universe for our well-being.

Rather than being subject to other people's expectations and my inner compulsions, I am operating out of a deep sense of God's call upon my life.

Rather than leading from a simplistic view of the spiritual life, I have an inside-out understanding of the shape of the spiritual journey that comes from having been faithful to my own journey.

Rather than arguing and fighting and trying to defend myself against every criticism and challenge to my leadership, I am regularly and routinely carrying the people I am leading into God's presence and interceding on their behalf.

Rather than carrying the burdens of leadership alone and being derailed by isolation, I am opening my loneliness to God and to those with whom I can cultivate a healthy interdependence.

And rather than leading from a place of intellectual striving and human strategies, I am discovering with a few others how to open to the gift of discernment so that we can do God's will together.

THE SEASON OF LETTING GO

But there is one more season of leadership when we can feel things starting to shift and we realize that maybe we are not going to see all our

dreams come true. Some of the things we had hoped for have come
about, but many have not. God starts to talk to us in subtle or not-so-
subtle ways about the fact that a change is coming and he is drawing
us more completely to himself. As the old hymn goes, "the things of
earth will grow strangely dim" as the presence of God becomes more
and more real.

This is the time when we might give our retrospective as Moses did
in the book of Deuteronomy, summarizing lessons learned and battles
fought, telling stories that inspire, offering wisdom and instruction
from years of leadership experience. It is time to give blessing to those
who will go on without us and to encourage and empower those who
will lead. All of these things we do to the best of our ability knowing
that they are an important part of leadership. But at the same time there
is something very intimate going on between us and God. There is one
more moment that has to be navigated, one more letting go.

Moses' ultimate letting go into the presence of God took place on the
highest peak of Mount Nebo, where God guided him to go and survey
the Promised Land one last time. He was 120 years old but his vigor was
unimpaired, the Scriptures say. He was still able to climb mountains!

Since my Sunday school days I have known the end of Moses' story:
he got to see the Promised Land but he didn't get to go in. Since Sunday school days I have understood that this was Moses' punishment for
striking the rock at Meribah rather than just speaking to it as God had
instructed him. Back then I accepted this as the consequence for Moses'
sin and allowed myself only a vague sense that perhaps it seemed a little
harsh. But more recently I have had to admit that it seems inordinately
cruel. The words God spoke to Moses as he looked out on what might
have been—"I have let you see it with your eyes, but you shall not cross
over"—seem like the coldest, most punishing, most withholding words
that could ever be uttered to one who had been so faithful. And God's
instruction for him to ascend to the top of Mount Nebo and look at the
land before dying seemed a little bit like rubbing Moses' nose in it.

It has taken me a long time to really face this part of Moses' story and look at it unflinchingly because it brings up a painful possibility—the possibility that this could happen to me. That I, too, could work hard and serve long—straining toward some goal or dream—and that God might someday say to me, "You can look, but you can't go in. You can long for it, but someone else will take it across the finish line. You might be the one who saw it, but someone else will take it the rest of the way." For anyone who has dreamed dreams and seen visions, this possibility is almost too much to bear.

This part of Moses' story does speak to the fact that when you choose the spiritual life the stakes get higher and higher. Behavior and attitudes that were good enough last year may not be good enough this year. A level of integrity that was good enough for one level of spiritual leadership disappoints others and yourself as you move into greater responsibility. There is a peace on this path and very deep rewards, but there is an even greater need to live authentically and more given over to grace. The more spiritual the destination the greater the importance of our character and our utter responsiveness to God in the journey is. There is a price to be paid for leadership, and I think somehow Moses knew this and had accepted it.

Even so, I have read and reread the book of Deuteronomy looking for some evidence of an inner struggle, some indication that Moses argued with God one more time on the side of that mountain. One thing we can feel pretty certain about is that if Moses felt like arguing, he probably would have! But I don't think he did. It is as if everything Moses had gone through had prepared him for this moment. Whatever letting go he had done in order to leave the house of Pharaoh to find God—and himself—in the wilderness prepared him for this final letting go. Settling down by the well in Midian and being content to be a soul in God's presence had prepared him to sit on the side of this mountain content, once again, to be a soul in God's presence. He no longer needed any role or responsibility or task to define him.

Perhaps his experience of being called by God, of arguing it out with God and having him answer each and every objection with the promise of his presence, prepared Moses to say yes more easily to the calling that was before him now. All of his experiences of discerning and doing the will of God had brought him to the place where he knew, down to bottom of his being, that the will of God was the best thing that could happen to him under any circumstances.

Certainly he had some sense that the terrible loneliness he had moved in and out of throughout his life was now finally going to be irrevocably eradicated because physical death was the final transition into that pure Presence. Finally there would be nothing standing between him and the lover of his soul. And this is what I have come to see most clearly in the life of Moses: *for Moses the presence of God was the Promised Land.* Next to that, everything else had already paled in significance.

> *Everything in my life has brought me here.*
>
> RAINER MARIE RILKE

CROSSING TO SAFETY

As I have struggled to come to some understanding of this aspect of Moses' life, I have become convinced that the peace that characterizes Moses' response to God on the side of the mountain is actually rooted in the journey of encounter that he had been on all his life. The culmination of this intimacy was his experience with God in Exodus 33—34, where Moses went through a fundamental shift in his life as a leader, a transformation of the deepest kind. This was the place where visions of grandeur and the allure of greatness ceased to hold the attraction that they used to. This was the place where the presence of God became ultimate and everything else paled in significance.

Clearly something happened to Moses—he was so changed by the journey that he was completely at peace with himself and God. Nothing of this world had any hold on him at all. By this time Moses and God were like an old married couple who had loved and fought for so long that they had reached a deep level of understanding. They had been through so much together that now it was enough to sit and rock on the front porch of life, each one content just to know that the other is there. That was all it took to make life good.

And so I have wondered, could it be that the promised land is more personal than we think? Could it be that the promised land is less about a physical destination or anything that is outward and more about a way of life and being that enables us to worship and love God fully? Is the land flowing with milk and honey a metaphor for this way of life that is good and satisfying and enables you to be with God on God's own terms for you? Is it possible for a leader to have encountered God so richly that no matter what we are working toward here on this earth, we know we already have what we most deeply want—the presence of God, that which can never be taken from us? Is it possible to get to a place where we are so given over to God that physical death is just one more step toward the intimacy and union we seek?

All of the great heroes of the faith affirm that the answer to these questions is a resounding yes. Paul came to the place in his life where he was willing to stay on this earth as long as it benefited others, but the possibility of fruitful ministry or achieving some earthly vision was no longer the biggest draw. "For to me, to live is Christ and to die is gain," he wrote to the Philippians (see verse 1:21 NIV). He was willing to stay faithful as long as that was needed, but he had come to a place of such union with Christ that everything else had paled in significance: "If I am to live in the flesh, that means fruitful labor for me; and I do not know which I prefer. I am hard pressed between the two: my desire is to depart and be with Christ, for that is far better; but to remain in the flesh is more necessary for you" (Philippians 1:22-24).

Martin Luther King Jr. expressed a similar conviction in a speech given in Memphis, Tennessee, on the night before he was assassinated. He spoke of receiving a letter from a little girl after he had been near-fatally stabbed in New York. X-rays had revealed that the knife blade was lodged so close to his aorta that if he had sneezed, he would have died. King received letters of comfort and encouragement from around the world, but the one from this young white girl touched him deeply. *Dear Dr. King,* she wrote. *While it should not matter, I would like to mention that I'm a white girl. I read in the paper of your misfortune, and of your suffering. And I read that if you had sneezed, you would have died. And I'm simply writing to say that I'm so happy you didn't sneeze.*

King then recounted many reasons why he, too, was glad he had not sneezed. He described a litany of victorious events that he had been able to be a part of because he hadn't sneezed—"I wouldn't have been around here when Negroes in Albany, Georgia, decided to straighten their backs up . . . or when the black people of Birmingham, Alabama, aroused the conscience of this nation, and brought into being the Civil Rights Bill . . . or later that year, to try and tell America about a dream I had had."

"I'm so happy that I didn't sneeze," he said. But then he went on to say that something new had happened within him, something that put him in a different relationship with all that he had been a part of up until now. It just didn't matter like it used to! King alluded to Moses' experience on the mountain, and with uncanny foresight (which many feel was a premonition), his speech gathered momentum until it reached a crescendo.

"I don't know what will happen now," he thundered. "We've got some difficult days ahead but it really doesn't matter with me now, because I've been to the mountaintop.

"And I don't mind.

"Like anybody, I would like to live a long life. Longevity has its place. But I'm not concerned about that now. I just want to do God's will. And he allowed me to go up to the mountain. And I've looked over. And I've seen the Promised Land. I may not get there with you. But I want you to know tonight, that we, as a people, will get to the Promised Land! "And so I'm happy tonight. I'm not worried about anything. I'm not fearing any man! Mine eyes have seen the glory of the coming of the Lord!!" This journey to the mountaintop is the ultimate antidote to our grandiosity, if we will let be. It helps us find our place in the scheme of things lest we become overly inflated in our view of ourselves and our role in kingdom work. It puts everything in perspective and it is a perspective we need. A prayer written by Bishop Ken Untener in memory of Oscar Romero, archbishop of San Salvador who was martyred for his outspoken advocacy for the poor, follows this line of thought:

> It helps, now and then, to step back and take a long view.
> The Kingdom is not only beyond our efforts,
> it is even beyond our vision.
> We accomplish in our lifetime only a fraction
> of the magnificent enterprise that is God's work.
> We cannot do everything, and there is a sense of
> liberation in realizing this.
> This enables us to do something, and to do it very well.
> It may be incomplete, but it is a beginning,
> a step along the way, an opportunity for the Lord's grace to enter
> and do the rest.
> We may never see the end results, but that is the difference between
> the master builder and the worker.
> We are workers, not master builders; ministers, not messiahs.
> We are prophets of a future not our own.

For a leader, the promised land is something that you see and know and that can't be beaten out of you even when other people don't see it yet—even when they say it is impossible, unrealistic, idealistic. It is the phoenix that keeps rising out of the ashes of every failure. It can never fully die. But paradoxically, by the time a leader gets to this promised

land, it has usually been stripped down to its barest essence. Paradoxically, by the time you get there, maybe you can still see it—as Moses did
and as Martin Luther King Jr. did—but it doesn't matter nearly as much.
What matters is the presence of God right there with you on the moun-
tainside and being able to say yes to God in the deepest way because you
are not clinging to or grasping at anything. Having that happen inside
you makes you a leader who is free indeed. It makes you a leader with
strength of soul.

THE LONG VIEW

I have imagined that there was also a sense of relief for Moses when God
told him that this leg of his journey was over and that, finally, he could
lay down this burden that had at times been so weighty.

God had already told Moses that the people would continue in their
pattern of prostituting themselves to foreign gods and breaking the covenant God had made with them. Moses had been there and done that
and had discovered that being the leader of that mess was not all it was
cracked up it to be.

There is such a thing as the rest of God (see Hebrews 4:1-11), and
God had been pointing to it on and off in different ways throughout the
journey. In fact, the practice of sabbath keeping was a foreshadowing
of a more complete rest that was to come, and Moses was finally being
invited into that rest. I have even wondered if the fact that no one knew
afterward the location of his burial place—that this was maintained as
something private between him and God—was part of the rest that God
knew he needed. It was part of the reward for this great servant of God.
Moses' burial place would not become a place of pilgrimage or com-
merce as the burial places of some of the great ones have become. His
bones would not be uprooted and carried around as Jacob's bones had
been. He would rest in the deep peace of privacy and anonymity knowing what he most needed to know—that he had been a friend of God.

Never since has there arisen a prophet in Israel like Moses, whom the LORD knew face to face. He was unequaled for all the signs and wonders that the LORD sent him to perform in the land of Egypt, against Pharaoh and all his servants and the entire land, and for all the mighty deeds and all the terrifying displays of power that Moses performed in the sight of all Israel. (Deuteronomy 34:10-12)

Moses' friendship with God was one that continued into eternity. The next time he appears in the biblical story, it is on another mountain where Jesus had gone to pray with Peter, James and John. While Jesus was praying he was transfigured before them, and in the midst of it all he was joined by two men—Moses and Elijah. Scripture tells us that they "appeared in glory" and spoke with Christ about his departure from this world. A cloud descended and covered them and they were with Jesus in the cloud when God's voice spoke to the disciples and said, "This is my Son, my Chosen; listen to him" (see Luke 9:28-36). Once again, Moses was one whom God trusted with what was most precious to him.

Every time I read about Moses' relationship with God I am filled with longing, and it is not the longing to get somewhere—although there are always new places to get to. It is the longing to *be* a certain kind of person. A person who knows God. A person who is faithful against all odds and does not shrink back. A person through whom God can perform whatever deeds need to be done—mighty or otherwise—but also a person who can be just as content settling down beside a well or sitting on the side of a mountain in God's presence. Someone whose face shines because she has been talking to God. Someone whose every move is a result of an attempt to listen to God and then do what he says. Someone who, when God says, "It's time to let go; it's time for you to come home," easily lets go and rests in the arms of this One whom she has grown to love and trust with her very being.

This kind of leader is not perfect. But this kind of leader is a person who has been met by God, and *that* is where their authority comes from.

Most people seem satisfied with gathering their authority in the form of ideas, opinions, and quotes from significant sources. They might control their information in rather creative ways, but it is obvious that the authority is outside themselves . . . they are not themselves sources of power, energy or life. The authority that we need must be total . . . it must also come from our souls.

This is a leader with strength of soul—one who continually seeks God in the crucible of ministry and for that reason is able to stay faithful to the call of God upon their life—to do their small part—until God calls them home.

PRACTICE

Take a few minutes to sit quietly and let yourself be the one who is sitting on the side of that mountain with God, looking out over whatever has been your promised land and all that has brought you to this moment. What does this promised land that you've been moving toward look like from your vantage point today? What does God want to say to you about it? What do you want to say to him? Have you come to the place where you are free from your attachment even to this promised land, so that however God guides you, you are able to say yes?

■   ■   ■

God speaks to each of us as he makes us,
then walks with us silently out of the night.

These are the words we dimly hear:

You, sent out beyond your recall
go to the limits of your longing.

Embody me.

Flare up like flame
and make big shadows I can move in.

Let everything happen to you: beauty and terror.
Just keep going. No feeling is final.
Don't let yourself lose me.

Nearby is the country they call life.
You will know it by its seriousness.

Give me your hand.

RAINER MARIA RILKE, *RILKE'S BOOK OF HOURS*

AFTERWORD

Leighton Ford

It is a lovely late fall day as I finish reading Ruth Haley Barton's *Strengthening the Soul of Your Leadership,* one of those days that lends itself to musing and memory. And it is fitting that I am in Rock Hill, South Carolina, a place where I have learned a great deal about the life and the soul of leaders.

At nearby Winthrop University we gathered together young men and women for many years as part of our leadership development program. We taught about evangelism, about communication, about leadership values and practices. But what I most remember are the walks and talks across the campus with emerging leaders who wanted most of all to share their inner dreams and difficulties—the soul of their leadership. During those years I myself experienced in this place times of both great fulfillment and agonizing despair. And all of this led eventually to a sense that God was calling me to a new ministry of spiritual companionship and mentoring of kingdom leaders.

Also fitting as I write this is the place I'm at—the Oratory, a retreat and ministry center in Rock Hill that has become for me a regular sacred place of listening and renewal for my own soul.

Perhaps this is why I am so moved to gratitude today for what Ruth has written. Although we have never met, I sense in her a kindred spirit, and her book has become for me a companion on the way.

I hope it will be that for many leaders, like a young pastor who, at the end of one of our retreats, said, "I realize today that the best thing I can be for the people I work with is to be able to say, 'It is well with my soul.'"

For him and others like him I want to recommend this book. Ruth's style is warm and accessible. I like her insights into the inner life of the leader. I admire her love for poetry and prayers, which she shares in abundance. I am deeply grateful for the helpful practices she describes and recommends. But what draws me even more is that Ruth writes with realness and integrity out of her own intimate experience of the inner journey of a leader.

Moses is the biblical leader she has chosen as a model. I find myself musing, *If Moses read this book, how would he react? Would he be grateful? Surprised? Dismayed?*

Somehow I think his reaction as he read these accounts of his leadership would, over and over again, be, *I remember that! I recognize myself! That's how it was. She has caught me!*

But, more than that, Ruth has, in this conjunction of Moses and her own experience, caught me—and I think she will catch most readers.

I read here things that both sting and sing, thoughts like these:

You can gain the whole world of leadership and lose your own soul, your connection with deep places within where God's Spirit witnesses with your spirit.

I'm tired of helping others enjoy God. I just want to enjoy God.

What would it be like to find God, not lose him in the context of leadership?

In solitude we must stop believing our own press.

God is not in any particular hurry to get us to the Promised Land.

Oftentimes our feelings of isolation increase right along with our success.

And my own soul responds both with "Ouch!" and "Yes!"

But most of all I respond with "Thank you," because I am reminded here over and over that it was not Moses but the God who called Moses who ultimately got the people into the Promised Land. God was at the soul of Moses' leadership, and is at the soul of Ruth's and mine.

When I got to Rock Hill early this morning, I was feeling quite sleepy after many busy weeks. I kept yawning as I took time just to be still.

Then I walked outside and sat on a bench by the pebbled labyrinth prayer walk, enjoying the warm sun penetrating the cool air. I read a story about a disciple who asked his master whether there was anything he could do to make himself grow spiritually.

The master answered: "As little as you can do to make the sun rise in the morning."

Disconcerted, the disciple asked what then was the use of the spiritual exercises the master had taught him.

And the master replied: "To make sure you are not asleep when the sun begins to rise."

I think that is what Ruth would say about this book. I certainly would. Reading this book will not strengthen the soul of your leadership. Only God can do that. But it will surely help you to be attentive to the God who is the strength of your soul, and the heart of your leadership.

A Guide for Groups

The purpose of this guide is to encourage your leadership group to *create a process* for reflecting together on the soul of your leadership and to provide questions that will move you beyond mere conversation to honest, open, and soulful reflection and prayer. This will require a level of safety within the group that is more akin to spiritual companionship than a Bible study, a book discussion, therapeutic fixing or problem solving. Another option is to seek out a spiritual friend or two with whom you would like to engage as you reflect on what God is stirring in your soul as you make your way through this book.

The guidance provided here will serve either situation well and is intended to relieve busy leaders from needing to spend too much time preparing to lead the discussion. This means that the role of facilitator can be easily shared among group members who are all remaining attentive to their own souls.

I suggest beginning each meeting with three to five minutes of silence to allow the inner chaos to settle and to get in touch with your souls. You may want to light a candle as a symbol of the Holy Spirit's presence with you—individually and as a group. This guide also includes suggestions for concluding your time together using the prayers and poems included in the book.

Introduction and Chapter 1: When Leaders Lose Their Souls

In preparation for this discussion, it would be most helpful if participants have worked through the "How Is It with Your Soul?" assessment (appendix) and are ready to interact with it as part of the conversation.

Begin with three to five minutes of silence. The facilitator brings the group out of silence with prayer or by simply saying, "Come, Holy Spirit, come."

1. How do you respond to the definition of *soul* put forth here and the idea that your soul is "the part of you that is most real"? Do you typically think of your soul that way? How might it change your priorities if you did?

2. When have you experienced "loss of soul" or something not quite right at the soul level? Maybe you are there right now. As you read this chapter, what did you find your soul needing or wanting to say to God?

3. Which of the challenges of spiritual leadership (pp. 25-27) resonate most with you right now?

4. As you worked through the "How Is It with Your Soul?" assessment, which of the categories were you most drawn to consider? Which question or questions seemed to indicate a place where God was putting his finger on an area of your life that needs attention if you are to be strengthened at the soul level?

Note: In order for the group to feel safe, it is going to be important for each person to share what they are noticing in response to the assessment—at least to some extent. Depending on the size of your group, it may take more than one meeting for everyone to have a chance to share. Do not rush this one; the sharing that takes place here and people's willingness to walk into this kind of conversation will be foundational for the rest of the process.

Close your time together by having someone read slowly and prayerfully the poem "Holy One, there is something I wanted to tell you" (pp. 33-34).

CHAPTER 2: WHAT LIES BENEATH

Begin with three to five minutes of silence. The facilitator brings the group out of silence with prayer or by simply saying, "Come, Holy Spirit, come."

1. How do you respond to the idea that "all of us develop ways of adjusting and staying safe in the midst of whatever danger or difficulty is present in our environment" and that these coping strategies are developed unconsciously when we are very young?

2. As you read this chapter, what did God bring to mind (or what were you already aware of) regarding your own coping strategies and where they come from? What lies beneath those coping strategies? If you are not sure, ask God to reveal it—as you are able to bear it.

3. Where in your own life have you experienced the truth Paul expresses in Romans 7—that when we want to do what is good, evil lies close at hand? What was the result?

4. How are you experiencing God's invitation to freedom from the inner bondage of being subject to deeply patterned responses that used to be helpful but could cripple your leadership now?

5. What would it look like for you to take your awareness of your patterns and what lies beneath them into God's presence, as Moses did—to settle into this truth about yourself and let God begin to do his good work? How can we support you in this?

Conclude your time together by having someone read the prayer on page 45 slowly and prayerfully.

CHAPTER 3: THE PLACE OF OUR OWN CONVERSION

Begin with three to five minutes of silence. The facilitator brings the group out of silence with prayer or by simply saying, "Come, Holy Spirit, come."

1. What is your experience of solitude currently? Do you find yourself preaching solitude more than you practice it (be honest now!), or is it a regular part of your spiritual rhythms?

2. Which of the phrases the author uses to describe solitude—a lifeline, a place where we settle into ourselves in God's presence, the place of

your own conversion, a place of refinement, letting the chaos settle—
resonates most deeply with your experience?

3. Do you identify with any of the unconscious, reflexive patterns described under "A Look in the Mirror" (pp. 49-51)? If so, which ones?
   Can you start imagining what it would be like to let go of these?

4. Respond to the John English quote on page 52. When have you experienced what he describes?

5. Describe what inner freedom might look like for you; how you are
   being invited to "put down the gun"?

Close by having someone read the prayer on pages 57-58 slowly and
prayerfully.

CHAPTER 4: THE PRACTICE OF PAYING ATTENTION

Begin with three to five minutes of silence. The facilitator brings the group
out of silence with prayer or by simply saying, "Come, Holy Spirit, come."

1. Where in your life are you experiencing a longing to receive a word
   from the Lord?

2. As you stay in touch with your longing, reflect together on these questions (p. 62): *How much paying attention am I doing—really? Do I have
   enough give in my schedule to be able to turn aside and pay attention when
   there is something going on that warrants it? If I have been longing for a
   word from the Lord but haven't heard one in awhile, could it be because I am
   moving so fast that I do not have the time to turn aside and look? Do I even
   have mechanisms in my life that create space for paying attention so that I
   don't miss the places where God himself is trying to communicate with me?*

3. Is there any place in your life where something ordinary is being made
   extraordinary by the presence of God? How can you bring more attention to this to hear what is God saying?

4. How accustomed are you to paying attention to the times when your
   heart burns within you? Reflecting on John 10:10, 2 Corinthians 3:17

and Deuteronomy 30:11-20, describe a personal example of consolation and desolation. What wisdom and insight comes from paying attention in this way?

5. How comfortable are you with bringing this kind of attentiveness into this leadership group and its decision-making process? Perhaps share an example of a time when you tried this and how it went or a time when you held back and how *that* went!

Conclude your time together by sharing any ideas you have about creating more space in your life for paying attention. Have someone read the prayer on page 71 slowly and prayerfully.

Chapter 5: The Conundrum of Calling

Begin with three to five minutes of silence. The facilitator brings the group out of silence with prayer or by simply saying, "Come, Holy Spirit, come."

1. How does this chapter challenge your idea of calling—especially the assertion that we are called first *to be* the person God created us to be, then *to belong* to God and to cultivate our belonging-ness, and finally *to do* what God has uniquely created us to do? Which aspect of calling do you tend to focus on most?

2. What is "the story behind the story" that has brought you to your current expression of vocational leadership? What parts of your story are connected with what you are doing now?

3. Is there a place in your life where you are wrestling with your calling or resisting as Moses did? Which one of Moses' objections to his calling feels the most like what you are experiencing right now?

4. How do you respond to Tilden Edwards's observation that "calling is a much abused word today" that can be "little more than a pious euphemism for doing what we feel like doing"? (p. 79). When have you experienced this? How do you experience the difference between career and calling?

5. Recall your own experience of having God set you on your feet and saying, "This is yours to do" (p. 83). How have you responded?

Conclude your time with a few moments of silence for reflecting on the question: What is God saying to me about my calling? Then have someone read aloud the poem on page 85.

CHAPTER 6: GUIDING OTHERS ON THE SPIRITUAL JOURNEY

Begin with three to five minutes of silence. The facilitator brings the group out of silence with prayer or by simply saying, "Come, Holy Spirit, come."

1. In this chapter we explore the stages of the spiritual journey, using the Israelites's exodus from Egypt as a metaphor. The movements described here are preawareness, awareness, turning point, the wilderness/roundabout way, times of testing, seasons of waiting and learning to be still. When have you experienced one or more of these stages? Describe one of the major turning points in your life as it relates to your spiritual journey.

2. Which stage resonates most deeply as being where you are right now?

3. How do you respond to the idea that God is not in any particular hurry to get us to the Promised Land (p. 94)? Do you find this frustrating, hopeful, challenging? Something else?

4. On page 95 Ruth writes that Moses is now "a fundamentally different person" and describes the ways in which this is so. How are you fundamentally different now than you were when you first began your journey? How have you experienced God with you at key moments along the way?

5. Do you feel you have learned enough about waiting on God in your own life to call others to wait when that is what's truly needed? Is there any place in your life right now that feels like the "liminal space" Richard Rohr describes (p. 98)? How can we pray for you and support you in this waiting place?

Close by reading the prayer on pages 99-100 responsively. The facilitator (or someone else who offers) will read the verses, and the group will respond by reading the refrain in bold print. (Note that the response is taken from Psalm 139, so you are actually reading Scripture as you respond.) Read slowly so you can take in and fully affirm the great truths expressed here, allowing them to penetrate deeply and affirming where each person is on their journey.

CHAPTER 7: LIVING WITHIN LIMITS
Begin with three to five minutes of silence. The facilitator brings the group out of silence with prayer or by simply saying, "Come, Holy Spirit, come."

1. Have you ever had a more mature leader tell you, "What you are doing is not good," as Jethro did with Moses? How did you respond?

2. Reflecting honestly on the symptoms that indicate a leader might be functioning beyond human limitations (pp. 104-6), are there any that characterize your life right now? (For now, refrain from any problem solving and fixing. Let it be enough to simply acknowledge the truth of each person's situation in the company of others who are also working at being more honest.)

3. How do you respond to Bryan Robinson's statement that workaholism is an obsessive-compulsive disorder (p. 104)? How do you see this evidence in yourself and in the world around you?

4. Do you agree or disagree with the idea that when we refuse to live within human limits we may be indulging in grandiosity, willfulness and even narcissism? What happens inside you as you acknowledge this?

5. Where and how is God inviting you to the grace of living within limits? What is your response?

Close your time together by having someone read slowly the prayer on page 114. Leave a moment of silence at the end so that individuals can sink and settle into an *experience* of accepting who they are so they can belong more fully to God in all of their humanness.

Chapter 8: Spiritual Rhythms in the Life of the Leader

Begin with three to five minutes of silence. The facilitator brings the group out of silence with prayer or by simply saying, "Come, Holy Spirit, come."

1. Reflect together on "the bondage of busyness." Have you ever thought of your busyness as a place where you are not free? How does thinking of busyness this way affect you?

2. How do you respond to Michael Zigarelli's research on busyness among Christians and the vicious cycle he describes? Have you ever considered the fact that busyness among Christians (and especially pastors and Christian leaders) is actually a place of cultural conformity? What might it look like if we as individuals and communities of faith refuse to conform?

3. When have you experienced the truth that Jesus seemed to know about how quickly our passions—even the most noble ones—can wear us out? These days, do you see yourself bringing a frenetic quality to your work or the "steady, alert attention that is characterized by true discernment" that comes when we are more rested?

4. Which of the spiritual rhythms described in this chapter create within you the deepest sense of longing? What words or phrases capture your desire?

5. How do you sense God leading you into spiritual rhythms that correspond to your desire for a way of life that works? What would it look like for you to be more gracious and accepting of human limitations as part of living as a creature in the presence of your loving Creator?

Close your time together by inviting group members to close their eyes and have someone read "Sabbath in Late Fall" (pp. 136-37). Read slowly so you can each listen to the exhaustion, hunger, thirst and longing; allow yourself to feel your body and soul reaching out for time of a different sort, and envision letting go of what is necessary in order to embrace life-giving rhythms.

CHAPTER 9: LEADERSHIP AS INTERCESSION

Begin with three to five minutes of silence. The facilitator brings the group out of silence with prayer or by simply saying, "Come, Holy Spirit, come."

1. When have you witnessed or experienced the truth that "the leader always gets voted off the island"? How do the quotes from Edwin Friedman on pages 139 and 140-41 help make sense of this phenomenon?

2. When have you found yourself accepting the larger-than-life role of playing God in people's lives? What was the impact on your soul? How have you found ways to shut down the process of projection as Moses did?

3. As you read and reflect on the Scriptures that describe Moses' practice of intercession (pp. 142-43), how does that impact your perspective on leadership? What place does intercession have in your own leadership?

4. How have you been taught to understand and practice intercession? Does Ruth's description of intercession as being "weighty and burdensome" resonate with your own experience? How was the prayer practice offered at the end of the chapter the same or different from what you usually experience in intercession?

5. How has suffering shaped your leadership and helped you enter into the suffering of others? Do you think the people you are leading see you as a person who is regularly entering into God's presence on their behalf?

Conclude your time together by entering as a group into the prayer practice on pages 151-53. The facilitator will read the opening phrase of each prayer (*Loving God, I hold in your healing presence . . .*) followed by silence so that God can bring to heart and mind the names and faces of people you know. You can decide together whether you will hold those names in God's healing presence silently or quietly say the names out loud. After an appropriate pause, the facilitator will say, *"May they know the deep peace of Christ"* and move on to the next intercession.

CHAPTER 10: THE LONELINESS OF LEADERSHIP

Begin with three to five minutes of silence. The facilitator brings the group out of silence with prayer or by simply saying, "Come, Holy Spirit, come."

1. Which aspects of the loneliness of leadership seem to be most prevalent for you right now—the loneliness that comes from criticism and sabotage, the loneliness of being alienated and estranged from meaningful human connection, the loneliness of feeling disconnected from or abandoned by God, or the loneliness of carrying too much of the burden alone?

2. When have you felt the need to know God's goodness—not just for the people you were leading but for yourself? What did you do? How did God meet you?

3. How do you respond to the idea that any leader who cannot endure profound levels of loneliness will not last long? How have you learned to love your loneliness, or at least to be at home in it, as Moses did?

4. When have you experienced the difference between belonging to a group and belonging to God (p. 164)? What does this mean to you right now?

5. At the bottom of page 165 through the end of the chapter, Ruth describes a pivotal moment in the life of the leader, one that can lead to our own Exodus 33 moment. This is the moment when you experience the goodness of God in such a way that it brings you into right relationship to your vision. Have you experienced such a moment? How has it changed you?

Without trying to fix anyone or hasten the process of coming into right relationship with one's vision, let it be enough to acknowledge together the loneliness of leadership, to pray for one another as you are led and to wait with each other for the goodness of God to pass by. Have someone in your group read the Leonard Cohen poem aloud as a way of strengthening your ability to stand in your loneliness and let God address it (pp. 166-67).

Chapter 11: From Isolation to Leadership Community

Begin with three to five minutes of silence. The facilitator brings the group out of silence with prayer or by simply saying, "Come, Holy Spirit, come."

1. When have you noticed that your cynicism, anger or "blustering" is just a cover for the more tender emotions of sadness, despair and loneliness? What is it like to admit that? When was the last time you were as honest with God as Moses was in Numbers 11?

2. How do you experience the great paradox of leadership, that we can be surrounded by people and involved in important tasks but still feel so alone with the burdens we bear? Was there a time when you did not feel so alone? Is it true that oftentimes our feelings of isolation increase right along with our success?

3. Have you ever found yourself clinging and grasping unwisely at those who may or may not have the spirit to walk with you? How is this different from the shared spirit Moses and those who gathered around the tent of meeting experienced in Numbers 11?

4. As a leadership group, reflect on the opportunity to move beyond teamwork to community at the leadership level. Is this something your group would want to be more intentional about? Which of the values that undergird community do you already have in place? Which would you need to add in order to move in this direction?

5. When a leadership community is at its best, which of its practices do you find yourself longing to incorporate in your leadership group? How might this help you move beyond isolation to community?

To conclude your time together, have someone in your group read slowly the prayer on pages 188-90, pausing between the sections to let God listen to each one's beyond-words groaning. Trust God to make the needed shifts in each person's soul—the shift toward light, hope, friends and mercy.

CHAPTER 12: FINDING GOD'S WILL TOGETHER

Begin with three to five minutes of silence. The facilitator brings the group out of silence with prayer or by simply saying, "Come, Holy Spirit, come."

1. In leadership circles discernment is often ill defined (if it is defined at all) and may be viewed as somewhat mystical, subjective, and even soft. How does the definition of discernment put forth in this chapter (pp. 192-93) strike you? Take a few moments to discuss how you experience discernment in your personal life.

2. How do you respond to the idea that discernment is the heart of spiritual leadership and that a spiritual leader is distinguished by a commitment and ability to guide others in a discernment process? Do you feel your leadership group engages in discernment when faced with significant issues?

3. Many leaders shy away from using the language of discernment because they have seen it abused in Christian circles. Have you ever experienced this? How did that affect you and others?

4. Do you believe that "God's will is the best thing that could happen to us under any circumstances"? Be honest now!

5. Which of the dynamic elements that make up a discernment process feel familiar? Which ones are new, strange or forgotten? Which elements of discernment would you like to include or bring back into your process of making decisions as a leadership community?

Conclude your time together by mentioning any decisions you are facing right now as a group. Hold those in God's presence and pray the prayer on page 208 out loud together.

CHAPTER 13: REENVISIONING THE PROMISED LAND

Begin with three to five minutes of silence. The facilitator brings the group out of silence with prayer or by simply saying, "Come, Holy Spirit, come."

1. How has the choice to stay connected to your own soul and to lead from that place over the last weeks or months changed and even transformed your leadership? Use the descriptions on page 211 to prime the pump and help you to notice changes that might otherwise be hard to articulate. Celebrate what God has done and is doing in each of your lives!

2. Have you struggled with or tried to ignore the story in Deuteronomy 34 about Moses getting to see the Promised Land but not getting to go in (p. 212)? How do you respond to the idea that this is the culmination of the intimacy Moses has experienced throughout his life and transformation of the deepest kind (p. 214)? What longings stirred as you read this?

3. What is your promised land these days? How does it pale in significance when compared to the presence of God right here with you right now? What would you give to keep cultivating the kind of friendship with God Moses enjoyed?

4. How would you characterize your authority? Are you one who gathers authority in the form of ideas, opinions, and quotes from significant sources, or does your authority seem to come from within, from your encounters with God deep in your own soul?

5. What will it take—what kind of reorienting would be necessary—for you to be the kind of leader who has been met by God so that *that* is where your authority comes from? How badly do you want it?

As you come to the end of this group experience, don't see it as an end. See it as a beginning—the beginning (or the strong continuation) of your life as a leader with strength of soul. See it as the genesis of a new kind of freedom from your attachment even to the vision that God has given you, so that however and wherever God leads you will be able to say yes. Sit quietly together for a few moments, allowing each person to claim their longing, their desire, their commitment to seeking God above all else in the crucible of ministry. Close with a reading of the Rilke poem on pages 220-21.

How Is It
with Your Soul?

An Assessment for Leaders

And what do you benefit if you
gain the whole world but lose your own soul?
Is anything worth more than your soul?

MATTHEW 16:26 NLT

The following questions are designed to help you assess the state of your soul as a person who is involved in kingdom work. As we move through these statements together, you are invited to reflect on each question quietly in God's presence, asking God to help you to see yourself as you really are and your life as it really is. Then place yourself on each continuum as honestly as you can.

These questions and categories are not meant to produce guilt, shame, or a sense of failure. Rather, they are intended to help you be honest with yourself and with God about the state of your soul. This kind of truth seeing and truth telling is a first step toward ensuring that you *find your soul* rather than lose your soul in the context of kingdom ministry.

If you become aware of indications that you might be losing your soul on some level (in other words, losing your connection with what is most real), do not try to fix things or problem solve just yet. Instead, simply ask God, "What are we going to do about *that*?"

1. More and more often I notice that I am going through the motions of the Christian life—championing things I am not currently experiencing in my own life, manufacturing emotion that I am not feeling, engaging in kingdom action but aware that sometimes I don't really care.

    ALWAYS   OFTEN   SOMETIMES   RARELY   NEVER

2. I am aware of a nagging sense that something is not quite right, but I don't seem to be able to take the time or make the effort to look into it. The truth is, I'm not even sure I know how.

    ALWAYS   OFTEN   SOMETIMES   RARELY   NEVER

3. I find myself rushing from one thing to the next without time to really pay attention to what's going on in and around me.

    ALWAYS   OFTEN   SOMETIMES   RARELY   NEVER

4. I am keeping up with what my work requires, but deep down I feel that I have lost touch with who I am in God and what he has called me to do.

    ALWAYS   OFTEN   SOMETIMES   RARELY   NEVER

5. I am tired—not just physically but spiritually and emotionally. I don't really know how to get rested.

    ALWAYS   OFTEN   SOMETIMES   RARELY   NEVER

6. I am aware of an underlying irritability and restlessness just beneath the surface of my life.

    ALWAYS   OFTEN   SOMETIMES   RARELY   NEVER

7. I can't stop working even when I know I need to.

    ALWAYS   OFTEN   SOMETIMES   RARELY   NEVER

8. I have become emotionally numb—unable to experience a full range of human emotion.

    ALWAYS   OFTEN   SOMETIMES   RARELY   NEVER

9. I find myself increasingly giving in to escapist behaviors (eating, mindless television viewing, substance abuse, shopping/spending, pornography, etc.) or escapist fantasies—dreaming about being somewhere else or having a different life.

    ALWAYS   OFTEN   SOMETIMES   RARELY   NEVER

10. I do not have time for attending to my human needs—exercise, eating right, getting enough sleep, doctor's appointments and medical procedures, picking up dry cleaning, getting the car washed, making home repairs, etc.

    ALWAYS   OFTEN   SOMETIMES   RARELY   NEVER

11. My most significant human relationships are getting shortchanged.

    ALWAYS   OFTEN   SOMETIMES   RARELY   NEVER

12. I don't have time to regularly engage in hobbies and other activities that bring me joy.

    ALWAYS   OFTEN   SOMETIMES   RARELY   NEVER

13. I find myself hoarding energy—avoiding people in the grocery store, holing up at home or in my office—for fear that routine social interactions will rob me of that last bit of energy.

    ALWAYS   OFTEN   SOMETIMES   RARELY   NEVER

14. My spiritual practices have slipped. Even though I know that practices such as solitude, prayer and personal reflection on Scripture are life giving, I find I don't have time or energy for them.

ALWAYS   OFTEN   SOMETIMES   RARELY   NEVER

15. I feel isolated with no one to fully confide in and no one who fully understands my situation.

ALWAYS   OFTEN   SOMETIMES   RARELY   NEVER

16. I am very good at seeing needs, thinking my way into solutions and making strategic plans, but I am not as clear on how to discern the will of God—alone or together with other leaders. Aside from what sometimes feel like perfunctory prayers for wisdom, we don't have a clearly articulated practice for seeking God's will together.

ALWAYS   OFTEN   SOMETIMES   RARELY   NEVER

17. It has been a long time since I have felt connected with the presence of God in my own life beyond what I am accomplishing for God and for others. Sometimes I suspect that my vision for the promised land of how I/we are going to make a difference in the world has become more important to me than my own relationship with God.

ALWAYS   OFTEN   SOMETIMES   RARELY   NEVER

On the day I called, you answered me,

you increased my strength of soul.

PSALM 138:3

GRATITUDES

Everything in my life has brought me here.

RAINER MARIA RILKE

This book is dedicated to my parents, who have lived their entire lives in faithful response to God's call. Because of them I have never known any other way to live, and without them my life in ministry would have looked very different. Twenty-seven years ago when I was a senior in college, they made the choice to move our family to the college town where I was going to school so that they could be near me and the young man I would eventually marry. They have lived there ever since and, it turns out, so have we. This life-shaping choice, made so many years ago, means that we have lived together in the same town all these years; they have been a constant loving and supportive presence to me, to Chris and to our children in the midst of life's many demands. My gratitude and indebtedness to them are unbounded.

I am full of gratitude to my husband, Chris, and our children—Charity (and Kyle), Bethany (and Ryan), and Haley—who endured the long and difficult season of writing that this work required. Thank you for your prayers, your patience and your gentle inquiries into my progress; your kindness spoke volumes about your love and care for me. Special thanks to Haley, the last of our children living at home during the writing of this book. Even during this intense season, we discovered all sorts of creative ways for grabbing time together, and what a joy it has been!

And to my brothers, Rev. Jonathan Taylor Haley and Fr. William R. L. Haley. You have been Aaron and Hur to me—supporting me and holding up my arms in prayer when I have been so weary and disillusioned that I felt I could not go on. We are bound together by blood and by a shared Spirit. Thanks be to God.

I am deeply grateful for those who serve and lead with me in the Transforming Center—especially Joe Sherman, Herb Hillabrand, Jonathan Taylor Haley, Rory Noland, Cole Griffin, and Dave and Dalene Strieff. Thank you for being willing to keep seeking God together in the crucible of this ministry. Thank you for staying faithful to this journey of love, trust and being given over to God. Thank you for your generosity of spirit in bringing your authentic selves to this work. Special thanks to Dalene for literally holding my professional life together while I kept going underground to write. And to Joe for being a committed friend and ministry partner all these years. It is no small thing!

Special thanks are due to my friends at InterVarsity. To Cindy Bunch, for guiding such a careful editorial process. To Jeff Crosby, for engaging my work both personally and as a marketing professional. And to Bob Fryling, for your ongoing commitment to me as an author and as a person in ministry.

As I wrote this book, I was also aware of my deep gratitude and respect for all the pastors, ministry and business leaders who have allowed me the privilege of accompanying them in some way on their spiritual journeys. Your willingness to share your lives so honestly and with such courage has convinced me that what is most personal is, indeed, most universal. Time and again, you have inspired me to be more honest and more tenacious in seeking God in my own life. May we also be known as friends of God.

Ruth Haley Barton
Spring 2008

NOTES

Introduction

p. 13   When I refer to the soul: Will Hernandez identifies "the use of the term *soul* holistically as the very 'essence of a person in his or her wholeness.' Psychiatrist-turned-spiritual director Gerald May basically concluded that soul is 'who a person most deeply is: the essential spiritual nature of a human being.' In short, ' "soul" signifies the whole person: thoughts, feelings, and movements of the will.'

"Biblically and theologically, the reality of the soul represents the *self* 'as nurtured and sustained in the life of God.' As both ontologically substantive in their formation and development, *soul* and *self* can thus be viewed almost synonymously. .

"The primary identity of the soul, then, as employed in this book is in direct reference to the totality of the person created in the image of God—'a valued, valuing, and valuable being' " (Will Hernandez, *Henri Nouwen and Soul Care: A Ministry of Integration* [Mahwah, N.J.: Paulist Press, 2008], pp. 8-10).

p. 13   "Soul slips away easily": Gordon Cosby, *Good Is a Timely Word: From the Preaching of Gordon Cosby,* comp. Peter Renner (Nowra, Australia: Moonchpa Publishing, 2001).

p. 16   *Crucible:* "Crucible," *Encarta World English Dictionary*, North American Edition.

p. 20   Ted Loder, *My Heart in My Mouth* (Philadelphia: Innisfree Press, 2004), p. 50.

Chapter 1: When Leaders Lose Their Souls

p. 23   "Many of the things": Barbara Brown Taylor, *Leaving Church* (New York: HarperSanFrancisco, 2006), pp. 101-2.

p. 26   "The soul is like a wild animal": Parker Palmer, *A Hidden Wholeness: The Journey Toward an Undivided Life* (San Francisco: Jossey-Bass, 2004), p. 58.

p. 27   "Emotional tension can always": Peter Senge, *The Fifth Discipline* (New York: Doubleday, 1990), p. 152.

pp. 33-34   "Holy One": Ted Loder, *Guerrillas of Grace* (Philadelphia: Innisfree, 1984), pp. 60-62.

Chapter 2: What Lies Beneath

p. 41   writings of Teresa of Ávila: John Welch, *Spiritual Pilgrims* (New York: Paulist Press, 1982), pp. 61, 65.

p. 42   "The dark side is actually": Gary McIntosh and Samuel Rima, *Overcoming the Dark Side of Leadership* (Grand Rapids: Baker, 1997), p. 22.

p. 43   "the personal insecurities": Ibid., pp. 11-12.

p. 45   "O God": Ted Loder, *Guerrillas of Grace* (Philadelphia: Innisfree, 1984), p. 86.

Chapter 3: The Place of Our Own Conversion

p. 48   "A leader is a person": Parker Palmer, "Leading from Within: Reflections on Spirituality and Leadership," address given at the annual celebration dinner of the Indiana Office of Campus Ministries, March 1990.

pp. 48-49   "The perception that": Paul M. Fick, *The Dysfunctional President: Inside the Mind of Bill Clinton* (New York: Carol, 1995), p. 42.

p. 53   "The purgative way": Alan Jones, *Soul Making* (San Francisco: HarperSanFrancisco, 1985), pp. 169-71.

p. 53   "movement to a fully integrated": Ibid., p. 161.

pp. 57-58   "O God, gather me": Ted Loder, *Guerrillas of Grace* (Philadelphia: Innisfree, 1984), p. 71.

Chapter 4: The Practice of Paying Attention

pp. 62-63   "In a profound way": Elizabeth Dreyer, *Earth Crammed with Heaven* (New York: Paulist Press, 1994), p. 23.

p. 71   "O God, let something": Ted Loder, *Guerrillas of Grace* (Philadelphia: Innisfree, 1984), p. 87.

Chapter 5: The Conundrum of Calling

p. 75   "When asked what motivates them": Bill George with Peter Sims, *True North: Discover Your Authentic Leadership* (San Francisco: Jossey-Bass, 2007), p. 8.

p. 75   "My inspiration": Ibid., p. 4.

p. 75   Schultz's calling is more: Ibid., p. 7.

p. 76   "Vocation at its deepest level": Parker Palmer, *Let Your Life Speak* (San Francisco: Jossey-Bass, 2000), p. 25.

p. 79   "Calling is a much abused": Tilden Edwards, from a lecture given during the graduate program in Christian spiritual guidance at the Shalem Institute, May 27, 1998.

p. 79   "Such decisive, creative naming": Os Guinness, *The Call* (Nashville: Word, 1998), p. 30.

p. 80   "Vocational calling involves": Tilden Edwards, from a lecture.

p. 83   "To the extent": Carl Jung, as quoted in John English, *Spiritual Pilgrims* (New York: Paulist Press, 1982), p. 131.

p. 85   "I believe in all": Rainer Maria Rilke, *Rilke's Book of Hours*, trans. Anita Barrows and Joanna Macy (New York: Riverhead Books, 1996), p. 58.

Chapter 6: Guiding Others on the Spiritual Journey

p. 88   Many of the places the Israelites passed through: I am indebted to Dr. Emma Justes of Northern Seminary who first taught me about the Exodus story as a metaphor for the spiritual journey.

p. 98   "a unique spiritual position": Richard Rohr, as quoted in a sermon titled "Living in Liminal Space" by Killian Noe, April 7, 2002.

pp. 99-100 "For the darkness of waiting": Janet Morley, ed., *Bread of Tomorrow* (Maryknoll, N.Y.: Orbis, 1992), pp. 22, 23.

Chapter 7: Living Within Limits

p. 104   overwork and workaholism quotes: Bryan Robinson, *Chained to the Desk* (New York: New York University Press, 1998), pp. 6-7.

pp. 110-11 "The narcissist has": Christopher Lasch, *The Culture of Narcissism: American Life in an Age of Diminishing Expectations* (New York: Warner Books, 1979), p. 91.

p. 111   "Since our churches": Donald Capps, *The Depleted Self: Sin in a Narcissistic Age* (Minneapolis: Augsburg Fortress, 1993), p. 9.

p. 114   "O Eternal One": Ted Loder, *Guerrillas of Grace* (Philadelphia: Innisfree, 1984), p. 26.

Chapter 8: Spiritual Rhythms in the Life of the Leader

p. 118   "It may be the case": Michael Zigarelli, "Survey: Christians Worldwide Too Busy for God," *Christian Post*, July 30, 2007, e-mail newsletter.

p. 119   "It's tragic": Ibid.

p. 120   "I discovered": Quoted in Wayne Muller, *Sabbath: Finding Rest, Renewal and Delight in Our Busy Lives* (New York: Bantam, 1999), pp. 5-6.

pp. 121-22 "Following a period of activity": Jim Loehr and Tony Schwartz, *The Power of Full Engagement* (New York: Free Press, 2003), pp. 29-30.

p. 124   "Right speech": Dietrich Bonhoeffer, *Life Together*, trans. John W. Doberstein (New York: HarperSanFrancisco, 1954), p. 78.

Chapter 9: Leadership as Intercession

pp. 140-41 "Self-differentiated leadership": Edwin Friedman, *A Failure of Nerve* (New York: Seabury, 2007), p. 247.

p. 145 "Cowardice keeps us": Thomas Merton, *Thoughts in Solitude* (New York: Farrar, Straus, and Giroux, 1956), p. 24.

p. 147 "The attitude of intercessory prayer": Rosemary Dougherty, *Group Spiritual Direction* (New York: Paulist Press, 1995), p. 14.

p. 150 "My father himself": Chaim Potok, *The Chosen* (New York: Fawcett Crest, 1967), p. 265.

p. 151 "A certain unavailability": Henri Nouwen, *The Living Reminder* (New York: Seabury Press, 1977), as quoted in *A Guide to Prayer,* ed. Rueben P. Job and Norman Shawchuck (Nashville: Upper Room, 1983), p. 122.

pp. 152-53 "Loving God": *Iona Abbey Worship Book* (Glasgow, U.K.: Wild Goose Publications, 2001), pp. 96-97.

Chapter 10: The Loneliness of Leadership

p. 161 "travel inward": Ronald Rolheiser, *The Restless Heart: Finding Our Spiritual Home in Times of Loneliness* (New York: Random House/Doubleday, 2004), p. 194.

pp. 163-64 "One of the major limitations": Edwin Friedman, *A Failure of Nerve* (New York: Seabury, 2007), p. 188.

pp. 164-65 "Our God Is Able": Martin Luther King Jr., *Strength to Love* (Philadelphia: Fortress, 1963), pp. 113-14, italics mine.

pp. 166-67 "Blessed are you": Leonard Cohen, *Book of Mercy* (Toronto: McClelland & Stewart, 1984), n.p.

Chapter 11: From Isolation to Leadership Community

p. 171 "After 25 years": Henri Nouwen, *In the Name of Jesus: Reflections on Christian Leadership* (New York: Crossroad, 1989), p. 10.

p. 174 "Christian community is founded": Dietrich Bonhoeffer, *Life Together,* trans. John W. Doberstein (New York: HarperSanFrancisco, 1954), p. 30, italics mine.

p. 176 "The written commitment": Gordon Cosby, *Good Is a Timely Word: From the Preaching of Gordon Cosby,* comp. Peter Renner (Nowra, Australia: Moonchpa Publishing, 2001), pp. 108-9.

p. 180 Scripture is read without comment: I am grateful to Joe Sherman, who serves as liturgist for the Transforming Center and has led us in developing our prayer rhythms and liturgies.

p. 187 "we need to find": Ronald Rolheiser, *The Restless Heart: Finding Our Spiritual Home in Times of Loneliness* (New York: Random House/Doubleday, 2004), p. 175.

pp. 188-90   "Hear me quickly, Lord": Ted Loder, *Guerrillas of Grace* (Philadelphia: Innisfree, 1984), pp. 18-20.

Chapter 12: Finding God's Will Together

I am deeply indebted to Danny Morris and Charles Olsen for their work in *Discerning God's Will Together*. Their work, more than any other, has shaped my thinking regarding corporate discernment.

p. 196   "As important as the practices": Danny Morris and Charles Olsen, *Discerning God's Will Together* (Nashville: Upper Room, 1997), p. 41.

p. 202   "God's will, nothing more": Ibid., p. 115.

p. 205   "this way of discerning": Ernest Larkin, *Silent Presence* (Denville, N.J.: Dimension Books, 1981), p. 59.

Chapter 13: Reenvisioning the Promised Land

p. 216   Martin Luther King Jr.: AmericanRhetoric.com.

p. 217   Bishop Ken Untener: JourneywithJesus.net.

pp. 219-20   "Most people seem": Richard Rohr, "Authors of Life Together: Inner Authority in Community," *Sojourners,* March 1981, p. 24.

p. 220-21   "God speaks to each of us": Rainer Maria Rilke, *Rilke's Book of Hours,* trans. Anita Barrows and Joanna Macy (New York: Riverhead Books, 1996), p. 88.

TRANSF⦿RMING RESOURCES®
A Ministry of the Transforming Center®

From Ruth Haley Barton

Longing for More

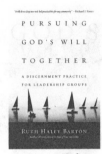

Pursuing God's Will Together

Invitation to Retreat

Sacred Rhythms

Sacred Rhythms DVD curriculum

Invitation to Solitude and Silence

Life Together in Christ

To see the complete library of Transforming Resources, visit:
www.Resources.TransformingCenter.org

TRANSF⦿RMINGRESOURCES

A Ministry of the Transforming Center®

Tools to guide leaders and their communities in experiencing spiritual transformation.

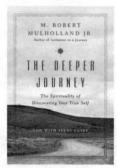

The Deeper Journey

Invitations from God

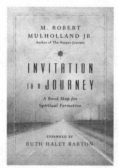

Invitation to a Journey

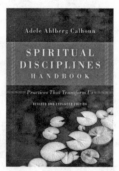

Spiritual Disciplines Handbook

To see the complete library of Transforming Resources, visit:

www.Resources.TransformingCenter.org

BECOMING OUR TRUE SELVES

The nautilus is one of the sea's oldest creatures. Beginning with a tight center, its remarkable growth pattern can be seen in the ever-enlarging chambers that spiral outward. The nautilus in the IVP Formatio logo symbolizes deep inward work of spiritual formation that begins rooted in our souls and then opens to the world as we experience spiritual transformation. The shell takes on a stunning pearlized appearance as it ages and forms in much the same way as the souls of those who devote themselves to spiritual practice. Formatio books draw on the ancient wisdom of the saints and the early church as well as the rich resources of Scripture, applying tradition to the needs of contemporary life and practice.

Within each of us is a longing to be in God's presence. Formatio books call us into our deepest desires and help us to become our true selves in the light of God's grace.

VISIT

ivpress.com/formatio

*to see all of the books in the
line and to sign up for the
IVP Formatio newsletter.*

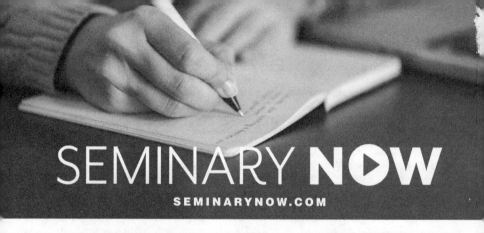

SEMINARY NOW

UNIQUE CONTENT AND DIVERSE VOICES FOR MINISTRY TODAY

A COMPANION VIDEO COURSE taught by the author of this book is available on the Seminary Now platform. Visit seminarynow.com to access this course and many others.

IVP partners with Seminary Now to produce video courses on select titles. Seminary Now is a subscription-based educational platform providing video courses on topics that help prepare ministry leaders for today's challenges.

SEMINARY NOW COURSES COVER TOPICS IN THE FOLLOWING AREAS:

- Biblical and Theological Foundations
- Old and New Testament Studies
- Church and Mission
- Ministry
- Justice and Reconciliation

AND EACH COURSE FEATURES CONTENT THAT IS:

- Accessible on most mobile, desktop, and smart TV devices
- Presented in short, 12-15 minute segments
- Offered in conjunction with a course study guide and assessment

To see the current course offerings or for more information on how to subscribe to the platform, visit seminarynow.com.

InterVarsity Press
ivpress.com